Testimonials

Diane Quintana's Now What? – A Simple Organizing Guide, which is filled with straight forward organizing tips and resources, is a must read for anyone that's going through a life transition. Her realistic approach encourages readers to work towards "functional" instead of "picture-perfect" organization. Diane guides you on your journey, as a calm, supportive advisor, sharing practical lists, personal experiences, and stories you'll relate to about organizing physical things, money, time and self.

Linda Samuels, CPO-CD®
Professional Organizer, Blogger, &
Author of *The Other Side of Organized*

"Now What?" should be subtitled, "How to be a Grownup" and it's chock-full of the kinds of practical advice nobody bothers teaching anymore but everyone needs to know. Diane Quintana walks the reader through all of the essentials of managing a robust, respectable life. Whether she's mapping out the intricate details of planning a move, creating an organized, live able home, preventing disasters in time and budget management, or offering sage wisdom on navigating etiquette, Quintana's wise counsel is specific, actionable, and creative. The upbeat tone of the book doesn't patronize the reader or mistake inexperience for lack of intelligence, and the resource lists are encyclopedic. This is the perfect gift for a new high school or college graduate, precocious teenager or any adult who hasn't quite gotten the hang of the grownup world.

Julie Bestry
Certified Professional Organizer®
Best Results Organizing

i

Who has not had a life transition? Even the most organized person can be overwhelmed by all of the decisions needed to be made during a life transition. Now What? Is an amazingly detailed resource guide with an incredible amount of valuable information. Diane has created a simple to follow step by step book, which can take a person by the hand through several transitions. Now What? will take the fear out of that process, and will make the transition much more enjoyable.

Cris Sgrott-Wheedleton, CPO, CPO-CD
Certified Professional Organizer
Certified Professional Organizer in Chronic Disorganization

Diane's book Now What? offers a comprehensive, step by step approach with practical tips for organizing. I especially appreciate the check lists and resources included throughout the book. In addition, examples of client and personal stories add meaning to each step of the organizing process. Now What? benefits everyone who wants to get organized, regardless of where you start on your organizing journey.

Ellen R. Delap
Certified Professional Organizer and Productivity Consultant
President, Professional-Organizer.com

Now What? is the book for everyone who wants a little more organization in their lives. This easy to read book has a wealth of tips and interesting anecdotal examples. Some of these ideas have to match up to just about everyone who is trying to make their home a place they want to come home to.

Jonda S. Beattie
Professional Organizer, Time Space Organization

Diane Quintana's book Now What? is chock full of personal stories and client anecdotes as well as specific (and quality) information about how to get and stay organized through life's often tricky and rocky transitions such as moving and having a new baby. Rather than offering esoteric, conceptual advice or platitudes, Diane shares specific tactics, techniques, ideas and great product recommendations that will help solve your biggest organizing challenges.

Monica Ricci CPO®
Speaker, Organizing and Productivity Professional

There's something here for everyone! I would recommend this book particularly for young people moving out on their own, or as a graduation gift. It's not just about organizing, it's a how-to book for some basic life skills. Follow Diane's advice and you will surely have a happy, well-run, comfortable home!

Hazel Thornton
Professional Organizer, Organized For Life

Whether you are leaving your parents' home for the first time or setting up your first home, this book is a "must have". This all-in-one guide is chock full of practical advice, organizational tips and helpful checklists. So much of this invaluable information is either taken for granted or never discussed. Leaving no stone unturned, the author's writing is easy to navigate and well thought out. Her own personal stories are the perfect touch for making her guidance come to life.

Leslie Josel
ADHD Specialist

I absolutely loved this book! Your organizing tips are easy, common sense, and practical to implement. In today's fast-paced and ever-changing world, everyone needs a place of refuge to think, relax, and just be. This book offers a sound approach on how to create that refuge. Kudos on a book that shows you how to live simply ... and live well!

Gayle M. Gruenberg, CPO-CD®
Chief Executive Organizer
Let's Get Organized

Now What?
A Simple Organizing Guide

Diane N. Quintana, CPO®, CPO-CD®

Now What?
A Simple Organizing Guide

To Kathy.

Happy Organizing!

Diane N. Quintana

Parkaire Press
Atlanta

Published by   Parkaire Press, Inc.
                      4939 Lower Roswell Rd.
                      Suite C-201
                      Marietta, GA 30340
                      770-578-1519

Visit the Parkaire Press website at www.parkairepress.com

International Standard Book Number – 13: 978-0-9818643-5-8
Library of Congress Card Number: 2014948384

Credits:
Illustrative photos in book: Jonda S. Beattie
Back cover photo of author: Tony Fiorda, di Sogno Photography, Atlanta, GA
Editing: Phil Locke
Cover Design: Main Street: Concept to Design, Pinehurst, NC
    http://rubiconfarmnc.com/msd
Interior Layout: Sanders Designs, Tucker, GA

Printed in the United States of America
10 9 8 7 6 5 4 3 2 1

Dedication

To the memory of my mother who provided me with an awe inspiring role model and who will forever live in my heart.

Acknowledgements

This book, *Now What? A Simple Organizing Guide*, takes some of the anecdotes I shared in my first book: *Flying Solo: A Guide to Organizing Your Home When You Leave Your Parents' Nest* and adds new information as I have learned a lot in the four years since it was first published. *Now What? A Simple Organizing Guide* would not exist were it not for my sister-in-law, Joan Norfleet. She has been there, encouraging me through every form this book has taken. She is a marvelous sounding board. I am very thankful for all the hours she has put toward making this new book a reality. I'm also very thankful to her for co-authoring the chapter on Organizing Your Kitchen. Her culinary skills and knowledge of everything to do with cooking is a huge asset to this book.

Thank you also goes to my cousin, Elizabeth Norfleet-Sugg. Elizabeth created these terrific covers and has been by my side encouraging the writing and rewriting of my book. She had tremendous faith in me and the message I want to deliver.

Phil Locke, my editor, was very tactful and patient with me as we worked through the chapters of this book. I so appreciate the time and effort he put into editing this edition of my book. Thank you, Phil!

Many thanks to Brenda Sanders for taking my plain text and jazzing it up with thoughtfully designed graphics for the interior of my book.

A huge thank you to Dan Pruitt of Parkaire Press for publishing my book and guiding me through this process.

A very big thank you to my clients whose trust and faith in me have provided me with experience and confidence to share my ideas in this book.

In life you never know who you are going to meet or the impact that person may have on your life. It was by chance that Maggie Jackson and I met at a conference. We had an instant rapport and I felt as if I had known Maggie for years instead of mere hours. There was no question in my mind about who I would like to ask to write the foreword to my book. I am indebted to Maggie for saying 'yes'. Thank you, Maggie for putting pen to paper and writing a fantastic foreword!

Foreword

The first image that comes to mind when I conjure up the words "now what?" is a fork in the road. We have all been there, either figuratively or literally, and we must make a choice. Robert Frost also comes to mind with his beautifully simple poem The Road Not Taken, and then I remember, "Both paths can be filled with wonderful opportunity!"

That is the beauty of this book. You are holding in your hands an excellent resource filled with choices to help you be successful during your organizing journey. The wealth of information in this book will allow you to seek out those solutions that make sense to your personality, your situation, and your goals.

We all experience difficult and challenging times. Diane does a fantastic job of providing you with many safety nets—what I often refer to as "Plan B." It is not only wise but also prudent to have redundant systems built into your plans—to have backup systems for just about everything. We never know when life might toss us an interesting curve ball. Being organized gives you a greater chance of catching those balls.

Diane speaks of our homes being our refuge. I agree with her wholeheartedly. Each day, we venture out into a world that is busy, chaotic, demanding, and sometimes overwhelming. To be able to come home to a calm and organized home is an excellent way to maintain a good balance and to support our mental and emotional well-being.

It is important for you to determine what brings you happiness Is it surrounding yourself with things—furniture, music, clothes, books and decorative items? Or is it having more time, more energy, more peace—all of which are promised outcomes of being more organized. Throughout the organizing process, you'll begin to see the value in surrounding yourself only with the things that bring you great joy. On a wall in my home, I have painted the following words:

"Have nothing in your house
that you do not know to be useful,
or believe to be beautiful."

This advice comes from William Morris, a late 19th century English craftsman, poet, and designer. I embrace these words in my own life and I strive to teach their meaning to each of my clients.

Diane has many excellent suggestions and techniques to help you take control of your belongings rather than allowing your belongings to take control of you. She will teach you to be aware of your surroundings. So often we stop seeing what is right in front of our eyes and rely too much on gadgets to guide our path. Take the time to truly look at everything around you because you may miss out on important chance encounters if you stop looking.

Life is full of chance encounters. Diane and I met by chance. We found ourselves sitting next to each other at a conference and I am so very grateful that our paths crossed. She has had a life full of organizing and her very own "now whats?" She has valuable experience and expertise to share with you, and reading this book is an excellent way for you to achieve your organizing goals. Diane has your best interests at heart—she is a mother, a professional organizer, and a seasoned traveler. She is, in my opinion, an expert on how to answer the "now what?" question successfully.

Remember to invite trusted family members and friends to help you answer the "now what?" question when you need help. Relying on the help and guidance of others shows remarkable courage and maturity. And it's always nice to have someone to guide you to choosing the right path.

My best wishes to you as you embark on your organizing journey!

Maggie Jackson, Certified Professional Organizer®
President and Owner of The Organized Life
Cedar Rapids, IA

Now What?
A Simple Organizing Guide

"The point of simple living, for me has got to be:
A soft place to land
A wide margin of error
Room to breathe
Lots of places to find baseline happiness in each and every day."

Leo Babauta
1973 -

Chapter

It's All About You

Many times during our lives we are presented with new and challenging situations. Some of them are of our own creation: leaving home for the first time to live on our own, marrying or moving in with a significant other, bringing a new baby home, divorcing or moving out of a living situation, or retiring. Some situations are not our choice, like dealing with the death of a loved one, or suddenly needing to care for an elderly parent.

Being a certified professional organizer I often encounter clients who are facing challenges such as the ones I've listed above… challenges that leave them wondering, "Now what?" Our lives are busy to begin with, and when you throw a life-changing event into the mix they become even busier or more chaotic. Whether you are a student, a stay-at-home mom, a working adult, a single parent, a newlywed couple, an empty nester, or a retiree devoting time and talent to volunteer jobs, our lives are so full that it is imperative to have a place of refuge that is free from the hustle and bustle of everyday life.

It's much easier to cope with life's challenges and remain calm when you are organized at home. I'm not talking about picture-perfect organization; I'm talking about functional organization. Why waste time hunting for a document, an article of clothing, the car keys, or your wallet? When your papers and computer files are organized and you know exactly where they are, then you won't waste time searching for them. Also, when clothes, shoes, handbags, keys, and wallets have places where they belong, you don't spend time wondering where you last saw them. It's the wondering that creates the feeling of anxiety… did you lose your driver's license or is it merely hiding in a drawer somewhere? The best idea is to have a place for everything and to put everything in its place.

When I work with clients, I present them with basic organizing concepts and then we work together to tweak the strategies so that the solution we come up with is tailored to their particular working, living, and learning style. Organizing is not a one-size-fits-all proposition. What works for you may not work for anyone else you know, and that can include people you live with. It is important that the organizing strategies you employ take into consideration the needs of everyone in the household. Shared living spaces can be organized in such a way that everyone feels comfortable, and your own personal space can be organized in the way that suits you best. Each of us is an individual with our own unique tastes and style. While the principals of organizing are the same, the way they are interpreted and applied can vary widely.

This book is meant to give you the fundamentals of organizing, and I'm not just talking about organizing the physical things in your home. I'm also talking about organizing your money, your time, and the way you represent yourself to others. I have outlined simple, practical steps you can take to create a well-organized and comfortable home and a well-organized and manageable life. I take you through the process of moving to a new home, setting up your living space, creating a budget, and organizing all the bills, papers, and other items that can so easily become clutter. In addition, I show you how to create, maintain, and sustain order in your busy life with time management strategies, basic cleaning tips, social etiquette guidelines, and even some recipes!

Keep in mind that when your life situation changes, your organization at home will need to change also. I revisit my own household organizational strategies every now and then and tweak them to better suit whatever is happening in my life at that time. Since life is not static and we, as human beings, are constantly evolving, it is only natural to assume that our home will need to evolve along with us.

How you use this book is completely up to you. Some of you will read the entire book from cover to cover, while others may skip around, reading only bits and pieces of different chapters. Do what works best for you. I hope you will be able to take the advice from the chapters in this book and interpret it to suit you and your personal organizing style.

My goal for you, my reader, is to give you basic tips and strategies to help you make your home the place you want to be; your place of refuge.

"Don't be afraid to give your best to what seemingly are small jobs. Every time you conquer one it makes you that much stronger. If you do the little jobs well, the big ones will tend to take care of themselves."

Dale Carnegie, Writer
1888–1955

Chapter 2

Organizing Your Move

Moving inspires both fear and excitement. It is the fear of the unknown combined with the excitement for what lies ahead. Of course, if you are simply moving down the street it is likely to inspire less fear, excitement, anxiety, and stress than if you are moving to a new town, state, or country.

You might wonder why moving provokes so many different emotions. It is due partly to the wide variety of things that must be taken care of in anticipation of every move. There is also an endless list of things that can go wrong. That is where stress and anxiety enter in—worrying about all the possible mishaps.

My husband Nick and I have moved transpacifically six times. Four of those moves happened after our children were born and so they were part of the move. We have also moved a number of times within the United States. Planning and organizing a move is now second nature to me. I vividly recall just how anxious I was before we moved for the first time. So if your stomach rumbles and you get jittery in anticipation of your first move, let me assure you that you are not alone.

Our first international move came the day after we were married. The wedding took place in Connecticut, we went to Hawaii for a honeymoon, and continued on to Bangkok, Thailand.

The bank Nick worked for was expanding their office in Bangkok, and they had asked Nick to be the Assistant Representative. It was a fantastic opportunity for a young man. Who was I to say that I wouldn't live in Thailand?

But I had no idea what to expect. As a young girl, I had traveled with my family, but never to Asia! Nick was not told in advance how long we would be living in Bangkok. All we knew was that we would be there for at least two years. Neither of us spoke Thai, and at the time (the late 1970s) English was not as prevalent in other countries as it is now, so the bank had arranged for Nick and me to be tutored in the Thai language.

All I knew for sure was that we would be staying in a hotel for about a week, and then we would be living at Nick's boss's house while he was in the States on home leave. While his boss was away, Nick was to manage the office and learn about doing business in Thailand. When Nick's boss returned, Nick and I were going back to Connecticut to pack up our belongings and really move to Bangkok.

On our second day in Bangkok, Nick went to work. Just as he walked out the door of our hotel room he turned to me and said, "Diane, why don't you look for a house for us to rent today? Also, you should start looking into the schools here. Maybe they have a teaching position for you."

I was an elementary school teacher and had just left a job as an assistant first grade teacher at a school in Connecticut. Honestly,

I felt like I could just cry. Where was the school? Was there a school in the area that used English as the primary language? Where was Nick's office? Could the two places be close to each other?

Nick knew that I got lost really easily. Very few Thai people outside the hotel lobby spoke English. Who would help me find my way? What would I do if couldn't find a teaching position? What other job could I find in this foreign country? All these questions and more were circling through my mind. I thought perhaps I had made a dreadful mistake. I was very young (23) and really was not at all sure how I was going to manage living happily in this foreign country.

After my little pity party, I told myself that, above all, I wanted to be with Nick. So I thought that at the very least I should explore the hotel. In the lobby there was a little gift shop. I found a Mary Engelbreit card there. The card has a smiling sun, a rainbow, a pretty cottage, and then this wonderful saying:

"Worrying does not empty tomorrow of its troubles, it empties today of its strength."

After I read this card, I made a conscious decision to take a deep breath and dive into life in Thailand. The office had arranged for a rental agent to help me to look for places to rent, and I found a beautiful home for us reasonably close to Nick's office.

As luck would have it, I found out that the International School Bangkok was looking for a first grade teacher. I interviewed for the job and ended up teaching at the International School Bangkok for 3 years—until we moved again.

Your first home may be across town or it may be on the other side of the world. No matter where it is you will have questions, concerns, and maybe some worries. As many times as I have moved our family I make the same lists. Your first move is the easiest and it is also the hardest. It is the easiest because you are probably only moving yourself and you may not have a huge amount of things to move. It is the hardest because having never moved before, you do not know what to expect.

What Do You Do First?

The first decision to make is whether to buy a home or rent one. Your home can be a stand-alone house, condo, or apartment. Ask yourself these questions:

- "Am I ready to be responsible for the roof, the on-going maintenance, and the yard?"
- "Would I like to be able to lock the door and not worry about the details involved in owning my own abode?"
- "Do I know the area well enough to know where I want to live for many years?"
- "Can I afford the mortgage payments?"

If you have any doubts, then you should rent. A lease is generally a one-year commitment, and the landlord takes care of the maintenance of the property. If the first rental doesn't work out, you can always move to a different area within the same town if necessary.

Whether you rent or buy, it is important to do some research before making your move. You want to be sure you are operating within your budget, so that's the very first thing to consider.

Figure out exactly what you can afford to pay each month for either rent or a mortgage.

You also want to feel comfortable in your new neighborhood. Drive around and locate neighborhoods that have affordable housing and the services you need: grocery, dry cleaning, maybe a park? You may even want to visit the neighborhood at different times of the day and night. Take a walk around to get a real sense of the place. Ask yourself if you feel comfortable. Recognize that you will probably not be living here forever, but you do want to feel safe and at ease in your new location.

Another thing to consider is traffic and mass transportation. Is this neighborhood in a convenient location to your school or job? Is the traffic such that you'll be stuck in it with a long commute? Is mass transportation available? If so, that will save you gas money, but how long will it take you to get back and forth and how much will your commute cost?

Know the answers to these questions before you sign a mortgage or begin meeting with rental agents. If you have a cat or a dog, find out in advance whether a rental property allows pets before you decide to explore it further.

If you are determined to buy, then do your research very carefully. Make sure you are investing in a good location. Also, take the time and money to have a thorough inspection completed. Talk to someone you trust who has recently purchased a home to find out the steps they took. You can also skip the next section...it's just for renters.

What Does a Landlord Require?

Every rental agent or landlord you meet will probably be eager to show you the vacant units available. He may even show you one that is larger than you need and therefore more than you can afford. He will definitely show you a unit filled with lots of natural light as this makes any unit seem bright and airy. He may spend quite a bit of time talking to you about the neighborhood and the facilities at the apartment complex. For example, the complex may have a fitness room, a pool, and tennis courts. It may also have a large meeting room with a big screen TV. Perhaps the landlord will tell you that residents sometimes gather to watch sporting events like the Super Bowl. This is all part of the landlord's job. He wants you to think that this is the place for you. To do his job well, he needs to have as many of his units as possible rented by qualified paying tenants. If you decide this is the place for you, ask to see the available unit. If you are a light-sensitive person, or if you like to have a houseplant or two, verify that the unit gets enough natural light.

A client of mine, Julie, was apartment hunting and saw a place she really liked. The neighborhood and location of the apartment complex were just what she had in mind, and the layout of the apartment was really nice. The sitting room was flooded with natural light because it had sliding doors that opened onto a small balcony. This also made the living area look bright and cheery. Additionally, the bedroom had sliding doors that opened onto the same balcony. The mistake Julie made was that she saw the model apartment and never set foot in the apartment she would actually be moving into. Since the price was right, Julie signed the lease. Unfortunately, it turned out that Julie's apartment had very little natural light, because the small balcony was covered in shade by lots of trees. Julie was very disappointed in that apartment and moved as soon as her lease was up.

You should also make sure that all the appliances are clean and in good working condition. Once your qualifications are verified, the landlord's job is done. All he requires from you now is that monthly payment.

The rental office may require verification of your salary. You can arrange for your new employer to write a letter verifying your salary to the rental agent. If you are a student, or if some of your paycheck is based on commissions, the rental office will probably ask for a guarantor of your monthly rental fee. The guarantor can be a parent, relative, or family friend who would guarantee to pay the rent in the event that you are unable to do so.

The rental office will probably also require a security deposit. This is generally one month's rent. You will receive this money back when you move out, provided there is no damage to the unit and it is reasonably clean when you turn in your keys.
In addition to paying a security deposit, you may need or want Renter's Insurance. Some landlords require this. The physical apartment or house is covered by either the rental agency's policy or the homeowner. Your personal property is not covered unless you insure it separately, and that is where Renter's Insurance comes in.

Renter's Insurance usually covers your belongings against fire, theft, and vandalism. It also usually provides liability insurance, which protects you if there is damage to another person's property while they are in your apartment.

Let There Be Light (Heat, Air Conditioning, and Internet…)

Next, there are the utilities to contact. The apartment complex or landlord will tell you what your rent includes. Sometimes the monthly rental fee will include the charges for water/sewage and garbage disposal. Look over your rental contract and if no mention is made of these services you should contact the rental agent and ask.

The utilities that you must contact to begin service are:
- Electric
- Gas—if the stove and oven and perhaps heat and/or water heater are operated by gas
- High-speed internet
- Telephone?

If your cell phone does not have a consistently reliable signal at your new apartment, you will have to sign up for a landline. Look around and compare rates. There are significant savings if you can sign up for multiple services from one company. For instance, if you sign up to have long distance & local telephone service from the same company that provides your high-speed internet and television connections you can save a bundle!

Keep in mind that the cable or satellite dish company will need to schedule a time with you when you have access to your apartment. Most of the time, the service person will need to be able to get inside to establish the connections so you will have Internet and TV services.

You will need to be at your new apartment to let the service person in. If you can't be there, you should have someone you know and trust to be there for you. It is a huge security risk to leave the keys with someone you don't know well. For example, you would not want to leave your key with a new neighbor you've only recently met. Your apartment superintendent or apartment complex manager will have a key, of course, but you must give them permission to open the apartment for any service personnel.

Furniture, Furniture, Furniture: What to Get

All right! You know that your lease begins on the fourth of August and you have set the utilities to start service in your name on that day. Now, you can decide when to move into the apartment.

What a feeling! It will be your refuge and your home – a place where you are in charge and in control.

List of Furniture:
- Bed
- Bedside table
- Chest of drawers
- Small couch
- Easy chair
- Bookcase
- Dining table
- 2–4 dining chairs
- Desk and chair
- Lamps

What does it look like? You know the floor plan; what sort of things will you want to have in your place to make it feel yours? Close your eyes and imagine you are already in your apartment. Think about the way you like to relax. Do you stretch out on a couch to read, watch TV, or surf the Internet? Do you like to lounge on a large beanbag chair? Keep these things in mind as you go about looking for furniture.

My younger son, Andy, lived in a one-room apartment for two and a half years. At the end of the lease, he fully admitted that he was becoming a little claustrophobic, but in the beginning he was thrilled with it.

Let me describe it to you. As you walked into the apartment, to the left of the front door was the bathroom door. Further to your left was the sleeping alcove. Facing you, on the opposite side of the sleeping alcove was a large walk-in closet; we put his chest of drawers in there.

To the right of the front door was the main room and living space where he had a small couch and a futon chair set up facing a bookcase with a television placed on top.

At the far end of the room was the kitchen area, which was long and narrow and had a cut through to the living space. Andy put a very small table there that ended up being a catch-all landing place for incoming mail, magazines, and other miscellaneous papers. He set up his printer and stereo equipment on a desk in the corner. As you can tell from this description, Andy's first apartment had everything he needed, even though it was just one room.

Be creative when you are thinking about your furniture. You can use a milk crate turned upside down for a bedside table. If you don't like the way the crate looks, but you still want to use it, put a thin square piece of cardboard on top to make the top smooth, and put a colorful piece of fabric over it. Put your reading material on top of that, maybe a small lamp, and you're all set.

You could make a bookcase out of a series of stacking cubes, or you could take a couple of narrow doors off of their hinges and set them on cinder blocks. When you build your shelves, keep in mind what you're planning to put on them—will they just hold books, or also CDs and DVDs? If the bookcase will also double as a TV stand, make sure it's strong enough to support the weight of a TV

Do you like to work at a desk? Desks are not the primary workspace for many people. I have plenty of friends who prefer to sit on a couch or in an easy chair with their computer on their lap, so I can understand why you might think you don't need a desk. But keep in mind that a desk is a good place to set up your printer and the wireless router for your computer. Since it probably has drawers, it is also a good holding spot for your printer paper, printer ink and other supplies. Additionally, it is a great landing spot for incoming mail and other print media.

If you really would never sit at a desk, then a second chest of drawers would also do this job well. A great resource to look at for decorating advice is the web site **interiordec.about.com**. You can find information on just about anything to do with decorating your home.

Furniture: Where to Find It

Now you might be wondering where can you find all these pieces of furniture at reasonable prices. I have several recommendations. The first is to ask your parents if they plan to do any redecorating. Our older son, Alex, got lucky that way. Just as he was planning to move into his first apartment, we were doing a little redecorating. He took a small couch that didn't fit in with our redesign. He also found a desk, a few lamps, and some other assorted items.

Places to Look for Furniture
- Department stores
- Garage sales/estate sales
  – Find information in the classioed section of the local newspaper
- Craig's List
- Church thrift stores
- Goodwill Stores
- Salvation Army

If you are not the fortunate recipient of your parents' extra furniture, you can look at the stores that sell good, basic furniture.

Always check out the auction houses, garage, yard, and estate sales in your neighborhood. These sales are sometimes also listed in the print or online version of the local newspaper. You can often find lovely pieces of furniture at affordable prices. The homeowner may be remodeling or moving to a smaller home and simply does not want to move certain items. Be aware that if you see it and like it and it is a good price (and it fits within your budget) you should buy it right away. Chances are the item will not be there should you decide to do some comparison shopping at another sale down the road. Don't hesitate to bargain for a lower price.

How to Bargain

1. Start by looking over the item.
2. Make sure you really want it before you start the bargaining process.
3. Begin by offering about ½ the asking price.
4. If the seller replies with another offer then,
5. You up your offer a little bit but do not just agree to the seller's price.
6. See if the seller will negotiate further.
7. If not, you have two choices: either pay the new asking price or walk away.

You never know if they have factored a little bargaining leeway into the original price! Also, always carry cash. Your credit/debit card will do you no good at all, and some people are really reluctant to take a check if they don't know you. While you may assure them that you have money in your bank account and that your check will not bounce like a rubber ball, they still may not trust you or be willing to take the risk.

Some department stores offer deep discounts on the furniture used as floor samples when they are changing the display. Ask the floor manager in the furniture department. Another website to look at is **www.1stdibs.com**. Sometimes they have great prices on quality furniture. Make sure to check out your local Goodwill Store and Salvation Army store, as well. As a professional organizer, I know these organizations are often the recipients of furniture and other household goods in very good condition that my clients no longer have a use for and just need to have out of their homes.

Other Household Needs

You will need other things to make your home complete. Things like sheets and towels are listed in the appendices. There is also a list called Essential Household Items in the appendices. It includes things like flashlight & batteries, candles, fire extinguisher, carbon monoxide and smoke alarm, garbage can, plunger—things that you don't think about until you need them! Staples for your kitchen pantry and other kitchen items are detailed in Chapter Four. Take those lists with you when you go to garage sales or when you are looking for furniture. You may find some of those items at bargain prices.

Moving Details!

This is where you should be careful to make very good lists. Everyone's list will be different. It will often depend on how far away you are moving. If you are moving to a new state you will have additional details to attend to. If you are only moving across town or even just a one-hour drive away, feel free to skip this section!

About a month or six weeks before you actually move, you should alert the following about your move, either in a letter, a phone call, or online.

- Post Office – fill out a change of address form or go online to: **www.usps.gov**.
- Banks
- Credit card companies
- Investment companies
- Insurance companies
- Medical/dental professional
- Utility companies
- Magazine and newspapers – try **www.oneswitch.com** This is a website that will forward your new address for free to all your periodicals on its list.

All the medical and dental professionals you use need to be notified in advance that you are moving so that they can get your records together and give them to you. If you go to their office, they will have a form you can fill out. If you do not have time to go to each of their offices, you can write one letter explaining that you are moving and that you will be coming by their office to pick up your medical records on a particular date, and send a copy to each office.

Many offices say they need at least 2 weeks notice. Be sensitive to the fact you are asking them to do extra work for you. Some medical professionals will only send medical records directly to other medical offices. They do not like to hand over the records; don't ask me why, but this has happened to us on more than one occasion. These records can be particularly important if you need to see a doctor or specialist on a regular basis.

My son Alex is allergic to bees and wasps. He usually carries an EpiPen just in case he is stung. This is a special injection to allow him time to get to an emergency room before his reaction to the insect's venom disables him. He has an appointment with the allergist every other week for an allergy shot. Those medical records are really important! When Alex went to the allergist about a month before his most recent move and requested his records, they told him to remind them at his next visit. He did as they asked, and when he moved he was able to present all of his inoculation records to his new allergist.

General health records are equally important because they include your blood type, your vaccination history, past illnesses and treatments, and any operations along with the outcomes. Even without the records, you should always know your blood type and when you had your most recent tetanus shot. It is a good practice to have an 'In Case of Emergency Card' in your wallet.

Information on Your Emergency Card

1. A list of prescriptions, including dosage & frequency
2. A list of vitamins and/or herbal supplements
3. Allergies, including contrast dye or latex
4. Any major surgery you have had
5. Doctors' names and phone numbers
6. Contact numbers for you, your health- care proxy or next of kin

Create an "In Case of Emergency Card" at:
www.realsimple.com/er

Now, what do you do if you don't know which doctor you'll be
seeing in advance of your move? Find out from your current
doctor how they would like to be contacted once you have
figured this out. Also be sure to find out how long your current
doctor's office will retain your files. This is really important!
Recently, Andy needed a copy of his medical records. I gave
him the name and phone number of the doctor's office in
Connecticut. He contacted the office and they told him they
had destroyed his file because they hadn't seen him within their
allotted retention time. In order to get the medical information
Andy needed, he had to undergo an expensive and time-
consuming medical test

When to Pack & How to Move

If you are just moving across town and have the luxury of being
able to easily go back and forth between where you live now and
where you are moving to you should probably skip this section.
If you are moving to another town, another state, or across the
country, please read on—this is for you.

First of all, you need boxes. Sometimes you can get boxes
at your local grocery store, but be careful which ones you
choose. You want the box to be able to hold your things without
breaking. Also, you do not want to pack in a box that is dirty.
Do not use a box that has food residue inside it. Packing boxes,
packing paper, tape, bubble wrap, and Styrofoam peanuts are
sold at U-Haul and Budget truck rental sites, and at some office

Packing Essentials
- Spiral notebook
- Pen
- Broad-tipped permanent marker
- Boxes
- Tape
- Packing paper
- Bubble wrap

supply stores. These items are not too expensive, and anything that is not used can be returned for a refund.

Boxes come in different sizes. Think about the things you are packing and how much you have of each category.

- Book boxes are small. Pack them with books and small items that can be used to fill the top of the box.
- Dish pack boxes are used for dishes, pots and pans, and linens.
- Boxes for glasses, stemware, vases—these boxes have dividers to separate the glasses and minimize the need for packing materials and the risk of breakage. You will still want to wrap each glass with bubble wrap. The difference is that after wrapping the glass it can be put into a divided section instead of carefully stacking the glasses.
- Wardrobes—basically hanging closets. These boxes are expensive and very big.

Wardrobe boxes are great if you have a lot of clothes to move and do not have suitcases or duffle bags. My personal preference is to pack the clothes in luggage, but duffle bags are wonderful because when you are not using them they can be folded and take up very little storage space.

Use your spiral notebook to make a list of the contents in each box. Label the outside of the box using your broad-tipped permanent marker with your name, the name of the room in your new home where the box goes, and a general description of the items the box contains. For instance: Quintana, Kitchen, Pots and Pans. This will help you tremendously when you begin unpacking.

Next, you need to decide if you are moving yourself or if you will be hiring a moving company. Moving companies can be expensive but reputable ones are worth the expense if you can afford it. The moving company will load your belongings into the truck and then unload at your new home and place the furniture where it belongs. Be sure to get estimates from a few different moving companies and ask for references. If you are moving yourself, you are going to need a truck. U-Haul and Budget trucks are easy to rent. Both have online sites that guide you through the process of deciding what size truck you need. The site will ask you how many rooms of furniture you are moving, how many beds you have and what size the beds are: twin, full, king etc. Some of the truck rental companies have a minimum age requirement. Check the website for that information.

Once the truck has been rented and the boxes are packed, you are finally ready to move. All you have to do is load the truck and be on your way. If you do not have strong friends to help you, then investigate further on the truck rental websites. Some of the rental companies have a service to load the truck and then unload at your final destination. This can be a great help. I recently used such a service when I helped a client move from one city to another. The two men came and surveyed the boxes and furniture. They took the bed apart, loaded the truck and made sure everything was secure inside the truck. The city my client was moving to was only about 45 minutes down the road so the two men followed the truck to the apartment. They unloaded the truck, putting the furniture and boxes in the different rooms, and then they reassembled my client's bed. The fee for their service was very affordable, and it made the moving process much simpler, which was invaluable to my client.

Moving Again?

If you find your needs have changed and you need a bigger or smaller home, or perhaps your company is moving you to different city, you should go through your belongings before you even contemplate packing. You do not ever want to pack an item that is broken or that has not been used in awhile. It could be that you don't even recall the last time you wore that piece of clothing or used that cooler.

If the items are in good condition you can itemize them for your tax records and then donate them to a charitable organization. There are many. Make sure you get a donation receipt to file along with your itemized list.

Even if you are not moving again, sorting through your things once a year is a great habit to cultivate. The sorting helps you eliminate clutter from your home. Do not feel you have to tackle every room or area in a weekend. Spread it out. Work on one specific area at a time. Designate one spot in your home to be the collection area for the belongings that are leaving. Decide how much time you are going to give to this task—maybe you will say that by the end of the month you will finish sorting through your things. At that time, take whatever is in the designated collection area to the charity of your choice.

Moving a Loved One?

Since we are living longer, it often happens that adults find themselves taking care of their parents as well as their children. What do you do if your parents don't live down the road from you? If your parents live in another state, what happens when you need to facilitate moving them so that you can oversee their care? This very thing happened to one of my clients, Debbie.

Debbie and her husband have three children and they are renovating their home a little at a time. This means that Debbie has to keep close track of all the children's activities as well as the scheduled renovations. Add to these tasks overseeing her parents' care and you know that Debbie has a very full plate. I'll tell you a little more about how she manages her time in Chapter Seven. Right now let's go back to moving the parents.

Debbie's parents lived in another state. So, for a period of time Debbie was making regular visits to her parents' to make sure that they were fine and that basic home maintenance chores and paperwork were taken care of. Flying back and forth between Atlanta and her parents' home became too time consuming and too expensive, so the decision was made to move her parents to an independent living facility within a thirty-minute drive from Debbie's home. This was a wonderful and freeing decision for Debbie. However, there was a lot of work to be done before the move could actually happen.

Debbie's parents had lived in their home for four decades. While the home was neat and tidy throughout, there were also closets and cupboards that hadn't seen the light of day for quite some time. The attic, basement, and garage also held 40 years worth of accumulated things. In addition to cleaning out the house to prepare it for sale, Debbie also had to help her parents figure out what to take with them to their new home in Atlanta.

Since Debbie had seen the apartment at the independent living facility and had the floor plan that included the dimensions of each room, she was able to guide her parents in the selection of which pieces of furniture to take with them and which to sell at an estate sale.

Debbie also hired a Certified Professional Organizer who worked with her and her parents to ensure the house was cleaned out in a timely fashion and then put on the market for sale.

It was great that Debbie was able to help her parents this way, but what if she hadn't had the flexibility to spend the time overseeing this move? There is an organization called the National Association of Senior Move Managers. They specialize in helping seniors move out of their home and into a new home that fits their current lifestyle. For more information about senior move managers take a look at their website: www.nasmm.com

Merging Two Homes into One?

It's complicated enough when you are single and are selling your home, buying a different house, and then moving. What happens when you and your partner each have fully furnished homes that you are selling and plan on buying one house together? Well, this very situation just happened to my friend Jennifer and her partner, Bob. In the interest of full disclosure you should know that both Jennifer and Bob are in their 70's.

As I said, Jennifer and Bob had fully furnished homes, so they had to make some decisions about what to keep from each of their homes. They certainly didn't need to keep duplicates of everything! Their first step was to figure out what from each of their homes they really wanted to bring to their new, shared home. Step two was to ask their children to come and take a look at their

> **Merging 2 homes?**
> 1. Decide what to keep from each house.
> 2. Invite others (children, other relatives, friends) to take what you don't want.
> 3. Take the remaining unwanted (but still usable) items to your favorite charity.
> 4. Recycle or toss things that are not usable.

furnishings to identify the items they would like to take for their own homes. There are some things that parents keep for their children thinking that they (the children) would just LOVE to have them. Often it turns out their children don't really want these items but feel obligated to take them because they don't want to hurt their parents' feelings. Jennifer and Bob were sensitive to this and didn't push their children to take any item they were reluctant to bring home. After all, no one should have anything in their home that they don't believe to be beautiful or want to use.

Then Jennifer and Bob took items to donation sites like Goodwill and the church thrift shop. Jennifer found out that the buyer of her house really liked some of her furniture and was interested in purchasing a few pieces along with some of the lawn care equipment. She thought it over and decided to sell these items to her buyer because they were keeping Bob's lawn care equipment and selling some of her furniture would reduce the overall cost of the move—an added benefit!

Jennifer and Bob successfully sold their houses and timed the closing of both to coincide with the closing of the house they bought together. They have moved into this new home, unpacked the boxes, arranged the furniture and are happy that they only kept what they really need.

"A place for everything and everything in its place."

Isabella Mary Beeton, Author
1836–1865

Chapter

Organizing Your Space

Defining Your Space

Prior to moving day, go to your new home. Take a walk around and really look at the space. If your new home is a studio apartment, think about how you want to define the space. How will you separate the different areas of the room? Will you put up a tri-fold screen, a bookcase (one that is open on both sides), a group of stacked cubes, or a solid piece of furniture to separate the sleeping and living areas? When you open the front door, what do you want to see first?

Look for electric outlets. The outlets will help determine where you place furniture that will hold electronic equipment like a television, computer, or printer. Think about these things, then put notes on the wall indicating the sleeping area, living area, and eating area. If you have actual rooms in your apartment, put the notes on the entry to each room. This is very helpful when the furniture actually arrives. The signs will remind you about where you want to put your things.

After the physical part of the move is over—the furniture is inside the rooms, and the boxes are placed according to the labels on them—the real work is just beginning. The furniture has to be arranged. The boxes need to be unpacked and removed. Then everything must be put away. Since nothing is familiar—this is a completely new space for you—you'll need to figure out where everything goes. This is a lot of work!

The Unpacking Process

Where do you start unpacking and how long does this process take? It only takes as long as you let it. Some people I know have taken months and months to get really settled in. They looked at all the boxes and got a little frustrated. It is daunting to look at stacks of boxes in every room when you just want the moving process to be over and done with. The last thing you want to do is unpack the boxes you have only recently finished packing! The boxes are labeled so you know basically what is inside. The temptation is to take a few things out of one box, put them away and then begin searching in another box for a specific item.

When my friend Clare moved to a new home, another friend brought her a housewarming gift of fresh flowers. She was thrilled with the flowers and wanted to put them in a vase, so she looked in one box and then started a second box and then a third looking for the vase. By the time she found it there were many half-unpacked boxes with packing paper strewn around. Then Clare couldn't decide where to put the things she had pulled out while looking for that vase. It took Clare many months to get completely unpacked.

Don't let something like that happen to you. Delaying the inevitable—unpacking the boxes and not deciding about where to put the contents—is counter-productive. Your mission is to get unpacked and settled as quickly as possible because then this new place you have just moved into will become your home and your place of refuge.

Unpack the Bedroom First

Start in your bedroom because moving is exhausting. At the end of your first day, you want to have your bed put together and made, the bathroom freshly cleaned, and most of your clothes put away. If you get nothing else done on the first day you will at least have a great place to sleep, towels in the bathroom, and clothes to change into.

Take a good look at where the bed is placed and make sure that it is where you want it. Is there an electrical outlet somewhere nearby so you can have a lamp on a table beside your bed? If your cell

Things to Put in Under-Bed Storage Containers

- Sheets
- Towels
- Blankets
- Out-of-season clothes
- Bulky sweaters
- Hats & gloves
- A small box of sewing supplies
- Extra bathroom supplies
- Wrapping paper
- Ribbon
- Gift Tags

phone is your only phone, where will you charge its battery? My son Andy also uses his cell phone as his alarm clock, so it is important to have his phone charging near his bed.

Move the furniture around until you are satisfied that everything is where you want it before you begin unpacking any boxes. Ask yourself if the chest of drawers is in a convenient place. Will it be easy to get the clothes out of the drawers? Step back and take a look at your room. You may even want to turn around, walk out of the room and then walk back in. Do you like what you see? If so, you are ready to begin unpacking and putting things away.

Unpack only the boxes that belong in your bedroom and put every item away if possible. If you find something that does not belong in your bedroom, put it aside and deal with it when you get to the room where it does belong. It is very tempting to walk away from the box you are currently emptying in order to put something away in another spot. Resist the temptation. Going to a different area is a distraction and delays making real progress in your bedroom. As you unpack each box, cut it down so that it lies flat. It will take up less space that way. Squash the packing material into garbage bags. Designate one out-of-the-way spot to collect all the flattened boxes. When all the boxes are unpacked, I recommend either transporting the flattened boxes back to the moving company or taking them to a recycling center along with the garbage bags filled with packing material.

Think Creatively

You may find, as you are trying to put some of your things away, that you need more places to put your belongings. Maybe you have more stuff than you thought. Also, the bookcase that you thought would work perfectly in the living room may actually have ended up in your bedroom. Things just turn out that way sometimes.

I have a small freestanding bookshelf that has often been in my bedroom and in one of our homes was in the kitchen. I would never have thought to use my bookshelf to store things in a kitchen but when it came time to put spices, condiments, and seasonings away after one of our moves, I didn't have a place for them. I did a little measuring and found that my bookshelf was a perfect fit against the wall in the kitchen, and that solved my problem. It gave me instant extra storage space.

As you are placing your furniture and putting away your things, try to keep an open mind and do not assign specific roles to your furniture. For instance, a chest of drawers that has always been in your bedroom and held your clothes may work great in the corner of your living room to store overflow kitchen things like placemats, trays, or casserole dishes.

Don't put things away just for the sake of putting them away. Group like items with like and put all of them together in a corner until you know where to put them. For example, if you have many more books than space to put them, you might consider hanging some shelves on a wall. Buying the supplies for the shelves and installing them will have to wait until you have the time and the money. For now, the books can remain stacked out of the way.

Also, you probably have a stapler, paper clips, printer ink, printer paper, extra envelopes, and stamps—items that typically go inside a desk. Perhaps your previous home had a built-in desk, but you don't have a desk in your new place. Where should you keep all your office supplies?

Keep collecting these desk items and grouping them together. When all the boxes have been unpacked, go back to your small piles of things and start thinking creatively about finding permanent homes for them. I say this because you want to be able to put things away where they belong, not in a temporary spot. One suggestion is to put a small collection of items into an appropriately sized basket, box, or container. The container can sit on a shelf with your books—perhaps acting as a bookend.

Use all available space. Is your bed high enough off the ground to have some containers underneath? That can be a great place for extra things like sheets, towels, blankets, or out-of-season clothes like bulky sweaters, hats, and gloves. You can also put containers of wrapping paper, ribbon, gift tags, sewing supplies, or first aid supplies under the bed. These are things you know you only need every now and then. They don't have to be front and center but they do have to be easily accessible.

Organizing Your Closet

As you hang clothes in your closet, remember to make good use of the vertical space. Get an assortment of hangers to hold multiple items. For instance, a suit hanger holds a jacket and trousers. A multiple-tiered skirt hanger can hold four skirts. I also recommend you hang categories of clothes together. In other words, hang all shirts together, all pants together and all jackets together. You can even take it one step further and group your clothes together first by category and then by color. It doesn't matter if you start with light colors and work towards dark or vice versa. That really helps save time when you are looking for a particular item.

Typically there is a shelf above the hanging rod in the closet, and sometimes there are two shelves. If there are two shelves put things on the top shelf that you don't need easy access to, such as extra backpacks, the empty boxes your electronics came in, or duffle bags. Use the lower shelf to store sweatpants, sweatshirts, a collection of t-shirts, handbags, and extra bathroom items. If you don't want to store sheets and towels in a container under your bed, the shelf in your closet is another good spot for them.

Closet Organizing Supplies

1. Hangers for suits
2. Hangers for multiples—pants or skirts
3. Belt hanger
4. Tie hanger—used for ties or scarves
5. Shoe rack—either over-the-door or free-standing
6. Shelf dividers—to keep items stored on the shelf together

If you have a lot of shoes, think about purchasing a shoe rack. A typical shoe rack can hold about 10 pairs of shoes. It either sits on the floor under clothes that don't hang down low, or it hangs over the back of the closet door.

Closet Organizing Tips

- Use the shelves in the closet for:
  - Sweatshirts, sweatpants, t-shirts
  - Sheets & towels
  - Extra bathroom items
  - Duffle bags, backpacks, handbags
  - Empty electronic equipment boxes
- Gather all ties & scarves and hang them on a necktie hanger.
- Gather all belts and hook them on a belt hanger.
- Hang suits on suit hangers and put all suits together.
- Hang shirts together.
- Put pants & skirts on hangers and hang them together.
- Put shoes away on a shoe rack.
- Make sure all hangers are facing the same direction! That saves space.

Milk crates are handy containers to use on the closet floor. Keep sporting accessories or maybe a collection of baseball caps together in them. If your closet is a walk-in closet, you may consider putting your chest of drawers in there. This is a good use of space if your apartment is one room and you want to have the focus on the living area.

The Bathroom

For your own peace of mind, give the bathroom a good cleaning before putting anything away. Some bathrooms have a small cupboard or closet in them. Use that space for towels and extra bathroom supplies. Roll your towels and then stack the towels by size and use. They take up less space that way! Store anti-bacterial wipes under the sink. They are handy to use when you just want to give the sink and vanity a quick cleaning. You can also keep bathroom cleaning tools like a toilet brush in a caddy under the sink. I recommend that you only put essential items on the vanity. This makes the area easier to clean and to keep tidy.

These are the things to be left by the sink:
• Tissues
• Soap either a bar in a dish or liquid
• Lotion
• Cup or cups
• Toothbrush holder
• Razor & Shaving Cream

I recommend that you put everything else away. If there are drawers in the vanity, use them to store other bathroom items. If there is limited storage space, you may want to get a small hanging shelf unit for the wall behind the toilet. You can find great accessories for organizing your bathroom and closet at The Container Store, IKEA, Target, and Bed, Bath & Beyond.

The Kitchen Is Next

The second area to unpack is the kitchen. Before you unpack any box in the kitchen, give the inside of the cupboards a good wiping down.

Check out the inside of the refrigerator, the microwave, and the oven. As long as you are making sure things are clean, you may as well clean these appliances, too, if necessary. The previous tenant or owner should have given the place a good cleaning upon moving out, but just in case they didn't, it's better to be safe than sorry. It would be terrible to put your dishes away in a yucky cupboard. In Chapter Four I will discuss how best to organize your kitchen.

The Living Area is Last

Let's go back to the original question: what do you want to see when you walk through your front door? What do you want others to know about you when they come over?

As you arrange your furniture and put away your things, think about that. Remember: this is your place of refuge. Let it reflect you. If you are a big sports fan and have a collection of sports memorabilia, find a place to display some of it in the living room.

If you are a photographer and have a collection of unusual cameras, perhaps you can find a way to showcase them. Maybe you collect literary classics and want to have a special bookcase devoted to those books. Perhaps in addition to collecting special things you are also a big music fan. You may want to print your current play list, put it in a clear plastic picture frame, and display it on a shelf or table. That way, when someone asks you the title of the song and the name of the artist you have it at your fingertips—literally.

Things to Keep in a Coat Closet
- Coats
- Heavy jackets
- Boots
- Umbrellas
- Tote bags for groceries

Make life easy for yourself. Designate a spot to put your keys. When you give them a home and return them to their home you will always know where they are. If there is a coat closet you can put a hook for your keys on the inside of the closet door. Maybe there is room beside the front door for a small table. You can put a bowl on the table and always toss your keys in the bowl as you walk through the door.

When you have finished organizing your home, and all the boxes and packing material have been removed, take a picture of each area. Do this to document what you have. Open the drawers, the cupboards, and the closets so the photos include small items as well as the furniture. This way you will have a visible reminder just in case you are the victim of a robbery.

Organizing Tips for Your Living Room

1. Use an old camp trunk to store extra pillows & blankets—it can double as a coffee table in front of a couch.
2. If you have over-sized books, leave them in a tall stack beside a chair.
3. Store DVDs and CDs in baskets and put them on a shelf.
4. Use containers—boxes or baskets—to hold small collections of items such as envelopes, pens, greeting cards.
5. Use a magazine holder for user manuals and take-out menus
6. Display your collection—whatever it might be.
7. Put photographs of friends and family around.

Make two CDs of the photographs. Keep one CD in a file labeled "Household Inventory." The other should go in your safe deposit box at the bank or another safe storage place away from your home.

If there are any expensive items, it is important to create a spreadsheet called "Household Inventory" and record that information. If you have a receipt with the date of purchase for each item, that's even better. If you have a scanner, scan the receipts and save the images on the CD with your inventory photos. Print the spreadsheet and keep a copy in your files, along with any original receipts.

Having a household inventory offers protection and peace of mind by providing a record of your personal property to simplify insurance claims, in case of fire, flood, or robbery. Remember that as you purchase new items and get rid of old ones, you will need to update these records. See Chapter Six for more information on filing.

Lingering Boxes

Sometimes, even when all the cardboard moving boxes have been emptied and recycled, not all containers have been unpacked. Picture this: you've unpacked everything except for a few Rubbermaid tubs that are full of odds and ends. In truth, you're not quite sure what's in the tubs but you feel fairly confident that everything you need has been unpacked and put away. So you stash these plastic containers in an out-of-the-way spot. Well, this exact scenario happened to a client of mine. Rachel called me to help organize the garage and finish unpacking some big Rubbermaid tubs that were lingering from her move six years ago. As we unpacked the items, we came across old phone chargers and lots of other odds and ends that Rachel felt were easy to either donate or recycle.

Then I found a small plastic bag that contained some brass pieces that looked like hinges or some kind of brass fittings. Well, you would have thought I found gold by the way Rachel reacted! She was so happy. She said she had looked everywhere for these pieces and was sure she was going to have to have new ones made. She explained that these odd-looking brass pieces were the clips that hold the dining table leaves in place. What a find! The moral of this story is that lingering boxes often contain items that you really want, and you'll never know unless you unpack them!

Respect Your Space

Whether you are living alone or sharing your home and expenses with someone else, it is important to have a discussion about respecting the space in which you live. Once the unpacking is finished, the boxes are removed, and your home is organized, the only way it will stay orderly is if you keep it that way. An unkempt home is not a peaceful refuge. Have the discussion with yourself and with your housemates (if you have any) about how you intend to maintain the order in your home.

If you have housemates, put together a list of things to discuss with them. You need to figure out how to divide the chores and the expenses. Some of the expenses are easy to figure out—when the utility bill arrives, you divide it by the number of people living in the home. Other things are not so clear-cut.

Be up front and honest with the others. Are you willing to share all the food in the refrigerator—is everything community property? If it is not, make those distinctions from the beginning. Perhaps the staples in the pantry are community property and the fresh food in the refrigerator belongs to the purchaser.

Make a schedule to rotate through the chores. Even if you are living alone, you should devise a schedule as soon as possible after settling into your home. If you have housemates, make the cleaning chore assignments so everyone gets a chance to take care of each of the chores. Remember to be a little flexible. Things will come up that make it difficult to stick to a schedule. The saying "if you scratch my back, I'll scratch yours" comes to mind. If your housemate doesn't have time to do their chore this week, you may consider doing their chore as well as your own.

If no one does it, the task becomes harder and takes longer to do the next time it is tackled. Maybe your housemate will volunteer to take care of your task the next time you have trouble fitting it into your day.

Different people have different standards of "clean and tidy." Some people can't stand to have anything out of place. Other people leave a little trail behind them when they come home: They close the door and drop their briefcase, backpack, or handbag, put the mail on the nearest flat surface, toss the keys somewhere nearby, and as they walk further into their home, their shoes come off and the person plops into the comfy chair in the living room.

Now, if that person eventually gets up out of the comfy chair and deals with the mail, finds the keys and puts them where they belong, puts their shoes away, and goes about their business, there would probably be no conflict. If not, there could be conflict if that person is sharing a home with someone who hates things in disarray. Talking in advance about how you want to keep the common spaces—the living room, kitchen, and bathroom—is critical to a peaceful living arrangement. After all, a battle zone is not a place of refuge.

Tweaking Your Space

As you know, life isn't static. Every now and then you'll want to do a little reorganizing of your things. From time to time you'll need to replace a piece of furniture, or you may want to display a different collection. Life events can also add to your belongings—you might bring in baby furniture for a joyful new addition, or mementos from a loved one who has sadly passed away.

I got a call recently from a young newlywed couple. Tom and Nancy have been married and living in a great apartment for a few years. They feel like they have pretty good organizational skills and were happy with the way their apartment was set up until Nancy's father brought over about 30 packing boxes!

I'm sure you can imagine just how overwhelming that must have been. Sadly, Nancy's mother had passed away and her father had decided that it was time to distribute Nancy's mother's things. So he packed them up and brought them over to Tom and Nancy's home.

Nancy was beside herself. She asked me, "Now what? How do I recreate order in my home?" We set up an appointment and then went to work.

We unpacked the boxes one at a time. It was clear that some of the boxes contained items that would be donated to Goodwill. Some of the boxes held knick-knacks that brought back terrific memories for Nancy. Of those knick-knacks, Nancy kept a few. She took a picture of the remainder and then put them in the donation box. The picture will serve as a wonderful reminder of the things her mother had collected without adding clutter to Nancy and Tom's home!

Other boxes were full of photo albums and loose photographs. We found a spot on a bookshelf for the photo albums. As we went through the photographs, we came across some that Nancy didn't want. She either didn't know the people in the picture, didn't recognize the place, or it was simply a bad photograph. But she still had a hard time discarding those pictures. After thinking it over and considering the space necessary to store all the photos, Nancy was able to let them go. If this quandary has occurred to you, give yourself permission to let the pictures go!

Try to remember to have nothing in your home that you do not love, use, or believe to be beautiful.

"Get people back in the kitchen and combat the trend toward processed food and fast food."

Andrew Weill, Scientist
1942–

Chapter

Organizing Your Kitchen

The Heart of the Home

My sister-in-law, Joan Norfleet, has a sign hanging in her kitchen that she picked up shortly after they moved into their first home. It reads "Gathering Room" and it certainly fits the space. Whenever we go to their home I always end up hanging out in the kitchen with Joan. She is a wonder woman in the kitchen. She has a knack for knowing how to combine flavors to create delicious meals that are not too difficult to make. Joan is also a wizard when it comes to knowing where best to put things in a kitchen so that it is well organized.

Joan and I often worked together when I lived in Connecticut. If we had a job organizing an entire house, I always asked Joan to make sure the kitchen was set up efficiently. I invited Joan to write this chapter to teach you how to organize your kitchen and to share some of her tricks for creating nutritious and delicious meals!

Our kitchen has always been the hub of our home. It's where our children, upon arriving home from school, removed their backpacks, kicked off their shoes, and had a snack while doing their homework. It's also where I would be: awaiting their arrival, prepping dinner, and inquiring about their day. We grew so accustomed to eating most of our meals in the kitchen that when I would ask my daughter to set the table—meaning the dining room table—she would automatically set placemats and utensils around the kitchen island instead.

With my laptop and wireless Internet I could be sitting in any room of the house right now but take a guess where I am? Yes, that's right, in my kitchen, sitting on a stool at the island, enjoying the warmth of the sun streaming in through the windows and skylights. In addition to working on my laptop, other tasks and chores I perform at my kitchen island include sorting and opening mail, paying bills, wrapping gifts, and even light mending of clothes. It's funny how much time I choose to spend in this room.

What is it that draws everyone to the kitchen? Is it the inviting aromas, or maybe the comfort we find surrounded by family, friends, food, and laughter? Whatever the reason, guests are almost always drawn to the kitchen. Many times guests will pull up a stool, sit down, and chat as I prepare a meal. Often they will offer to help, and we will end up side by side engaged in conversation while chopping vegetables. Dining at home with friends or family is not only less costly than dining out, it's also more relaxing and fun.

In order to work smoothly and efficiently in your kitchen, regardless of its size, you need to know where to put things. When there is a designated home for all your kitchen supplies, you never need to hesitate while working in your kitchen. You can reach for a potholder and be confident it is there. You can open a drawer and find the knife you need to chop an onion. When someone stops by unexpectedly you are able to open a cupboard without even thinking and offer something to drink and perhaps a snack. So, how do you go about doing this?

Where to Put Things In Your Kitchen

Make sure you keep items near their intended use. For instance, put your coffee filters in a drawer or cabinet near the coffee pot. Frequently used items should be placed on shelves in the front of cabinets and those used less frequently should be behind them. The same holds true for your vertical space. Put those items you use often within your reach, and keep those used less frequently up high (where you may need a step stool).

Pots and pans can be stored on a hanging rack, or on a shelf in a cabinet near the stove. Potholders and oven mitts should be near the stove, too—always within reach.

Glassware and dinner plates should go in a cabinet close to the sink and dishwasher.

If you have space between the top of your cabinets and the ceiling, think about displaying decorative vases, bowls, or platters in this often-neglected space. In our old kitchen I displayed a collection of handmade birdhouses and it added color and whimsy to our small white kitchen. Have fun and make the space yours!

Cleaning products can be kept in a caddy or tote under your kitchen sink to be carried and used where needed.

Go to your local hardware store, Target, Walmart, The Container Store, IKEA, or their websites to find organizing solutions for your kitchen space and needs.

To Maximize Shelf and Cabinet Space Consider the Following:

- Hang hooks underneath a shelf to hold cups/mugs.
- Think about using your space vertically—store platters, baking sheets, and tins on their sides. You can find dividers made for this purpose.
- Look for organizers that can be mounted inside a cabinet door to hold plastic wrap, foil, waxed paper, storage bags, pot lids, etc.
- Keep small appliances that are not used on a daily basis in a cabinet.
- Certain appliances (microwave ovens, toaster ovens, can openers) can be mounted under an upper cabinet to free up counter space.
- Keep your favorite cookbooks on a shelf or in a small bookcase in your kitchen.

Kitchen Shopping List

Here is a list of the things you should have in your kitchen. As time goes on you will want to supplement your collection with more specialized cooking tools, but for now this is a really good starter list of kitchen essentials. You may be able to find some of these items in your parents' kitchen, if they have a few extras floating around. Garage sales and estate sales are also good places to look.

- 3-quart and 4-quart saucepans with lids
- Stockpot
- Wok or sauté pan
- Small frying pan
- Utensils such as a long-handled slotted spoon, long-handled spoon, spatula, and whisk
- Measuring cups and measuring spoons
- 9" x 9" glass baking dish
- 9" x 13" glass baking dish
- Pie pan
- Broiling pan
- Roasting pan
- Cookie sheets (2 of them)
- Cooling rack
- Kitchen knives: paring knife, chef's knife, and serrated/bread knife
- Vegetable peeler
- Can opener
- Colander
- Paper towel holder
- Mixing bowls (set of 3 in graduated sizes)
- Ice cream scoop
- Airtight containers for flour and sugar
- Salt and pepper shakers
- Cutting board
- Salad Bowl and servers
- Oven thermometer
- Kitchen timer
- Dishes: 4 of each—dinner plates, lunch plates, soup bowls, cereal bowls, mugs for tea or coffee

- Glassware: 4 of each—short glasses, tall glasses
- Flatware: 4 of each—forks, knives, teaspoons, soup spoons

You may find as the years go on that you want more plates or serving dishes. Take time every now and then to go through your cupboards and assess what you're keeping there. You may come across small appliances, pots and pans, dishes, or glassware that you either don't like, don't need, or don't use. Pack these items up and donate them!

Refrigerator and Pantry Staples

Just as there are essential tools to have in your kitchen, there are some essential items to have in your refrigerator and your pantry. When you keep these items in stock, you will be able to make a lot of recipes using just the items you have on hand. Take a look at the two lists that follow.

Staples for the Refrigerator
- Butter: salted and unsalted (this can also be frozen)
- Milk
- Eggs
- Cheese: wedges and/or shredded
- Yogurt
- Mayonnaise
- Mustard
- Ketchup
- Jam/jelly
- Maple syrup
- Salad greens
- Fresh herbs
- Flour tortillas or wraps

- Bread (buy a good French baguette or a crusty ciabatta loaf and cut it into thirds or fourths and place in a freezer bag – defrost for a sandwich or to make crostini)

Staples for Your Pantry

As you put your pantry items away try and sort them by use, so you can more easily locate what you're looking for. For instance, keep all baking items together, all canned goods together, and all pastas on the same shelf. You should also repackage flour, sugar, rice, and grains into airtight glass or plastic containers to prevent bugs.

- Flour, all-purpose
- Sugar
- Salt: kosher and table
- Pepper (whole peppercorns)
- Baking soda (3 boxes: 1 for the pantry, 1 for the refrigerator, and 1 for the freezer)
- Baking powder
- Coffee and tea
- Pasta: spaghetti, penne, farfalle, orzo
- Rice: long grain, brown
- Couscous
- Oatmeal (old fashioned)
- Beans: black, navy, kidney
- Chicken/Beef/Vegetable broth or stock (sold in cans or cartons)
- Worcestershire Sauce
- Salsa
- Oyster sauce (found in International food aisle)
- Hoisin sauce (found in International food aisle)
- Vinegar: Red wine or Balsamic

- Oils: Extra Virgin olive oil, vegetable or canola oil, sesame oil
- Natural peanut butter
- Canned tomatoes: whole, chopped
- Potatoes
- Onions
- Garlic (can be peeled and stored in an airtight jar in the refrigerator so it is ready to use when needed)
- Nuts (for baking and/or snacking): to increase their shelf life you can put them in a storage bag and freeze
- Dried fruit (raisins, cranberries, cherries, apricots, etc.): also for baking and/or snacking
- Herbs and Spices*: crushed red pepper, cayenne pepper, chili powder, cinnamon, ground cumin, garlic powder, onion powder, oregano, paprika, dried thyme

NOTE: Fresh herbs provide optimum flavor, but if you don't have them on hand you can substitute dried. The flavor of dried herbs is more concentrated than fresh so you only need 1/3 the amount. If a recipe calls for 1 tablespoon of fresh herbs, you can substitute 1 teaspoon of dried herbs.

How to Create Simple Meals Using these Staples

It's easy to prepare a quick healthy meal when you have the previously listed staples on hand in your kitchen. When you supplement these items with produce and meats—such as fresh or frozen vegetables, chicken, pork, beef, or fish, you can make just about anything. With a bag of mixed frozen vegetables in your freezer you can prepare an easy meal of stir-fried vegetables with chicken or pork, fried rice, an omelet, or a frittata.

I've included a recipe for a delicious stir-fry dinner using either boneless chicken or pork tenderloin (cut and thinly sliced into strips) and seasoned with salt and pepper in Appendix C: Recipes from Joan's Kitchen.

Familiarize yourself with what's available in your local markets, and look for a seasonal farmer's market in your area and buy fresh local produce. Here are some good reasons to buy locally grown food:
- Save money (produce that's in season is always less expensive)
- Enjoy better taste and freshness (produce is picked at its peak, not prematurely for shipping purposes)
- Support your local economy and family farms (money spent goes directly to the farmer)
- Improve your health (by knowing where and how your food is grown, you can protect yourself from unnecessary chemicals and pesticides)

Whenever possible, BUY ORGANIC. We know that organic produce is not always available and can be more expensive than conventionally grown produce, but is it worth spending the extra money on? YES, definitely, especially for the items noted on the Environmental Working Group's list of the "Dirty Dozen"—produce that contains the highest amount of pesticide residue. These items include apples, celery, strawberries, grapes, spinach, lettuce, sweet bell peppers and more. To help you make wiser choices and reduce your exposure to pesticides use the EWG's "Shopper's Guide to Pesticides and Produce". For more information visit their site at: **www.ewg.org/Foodnews/**.

A healthy diet = a fit mind and body! After all, YOU ARE WHAT YOU EAT! Give your body the best fuel you can afford. Breakfast is your jump-start to the day. You wouldn't think of driving your car on an empty tank—why do it to your body? It doesn't have to be a huge meal—it could be just a small piece of cheese, a handful of nuts, and a piece of fruit.

Breakfast Suggestions:
- Eggs and cheese (not processed) are a great source of protein.
- Oatmeal is high in fiber and will keep you feeling satisfied until lunchtime.
- Fruit is always good. Enjoy what's in season and try to buy organic.
- Yogurt is delicious on its own or sprinkled with granola or fresh fruit.

Have you ever tried making your own granola? It's easy to do and you can customize it to your own taste. You can fill a bag and eat it on the run. Enjoy as a snack, with milk, on top of yogurt or vanilla ice cream, or with fresh fruit. There's a recipe for nutty granola included in Appendix C: Recipes from Joan's Kitchen.

I have put some of my favorite recipes for Lunch/Brunch and Dinners in Appendix C. I also included a basic no-fail chocolate cake recipe!

Looking for a new recipe? For some great inspiration, check out **www.epicurious.com**, **www.foodnetwork.com**, **www.delish. com**, **www.cozi.com**, or one of the many other online recipe sources available today.

On these websites you can find a recipe based on the ingredients you currently have at home, your dietary needs or restrictions, or even the amount of time you want to spend preparing and cooking the meal. Some sites will even put together a shopping list for you. When searching for recipes on these sites, take a few minutes to read some of the reviews. They sometimes offer helpful tips and advice for preparing the recipes.

How to Store Food Properly

When in doubt… throw it out!

How many times have you found something in your refrigerator or freezer and not known what it was or how long it had been in there? A simple solution to this problem is a permanent marker. Write the date (when opened) on the bottom of jars, cans, cartons, bottles, etc. before placing them in your refrigerator. When you store leftovers in your refrigerator, consider wrapping them in plastic wrap or placing them in a clear container so you can see what you're storing. You'll be more apt to use the leftovers (in a stir-fry, for example) if you can clearly see them! Also date those items being stored in your pantry—be sure to place newly purchased products behind existing ones (as they do in the supermarket).

Once dated there is no question as to the age of the item and when it should be used by or replaced. Spices, for instance, gradually lose their potency once opened. Purchase the smallest possible quantity of spices you rarely use and replace them after a year. Buy the larger, more economical size of spices you use often. If you get into the habit of dating everything you eliminate guesswork and waste. This also applies to your freezer—

anything that goes into a storage bag or container should be labeled and dated.

How long can you safely store food in the refrigerator? The chart on the next page shows recommended time frames for cold storage items.

This is only a partial list. For a complete list go to www.fightbac.org created by The Partnership for Food Safety, or check www.fsis.usda.gov, the USDA Food Safety and Inspection Service.

Once a week, do a clean sweep; remove expired and questionable from of your refrigerator. Always remember—when in doubt, throw it out! It is better to be safe than sorry.

Food Safety Guidelines

Keep food safe by following these guidelines, as outlined by the Partnership for Food Safety Education:

Raw and cooked food may not be safe after sitting out at room temperature for more than two hours. Follow the "two hour rule," and toss perishable foods left out for longer than that.
- Always wash hands with soap and warm water before and after handling food.
- Use one cutting board for fresh produce and a separate one for raw meat, poultry, and seafood.
- Wash cutting boards, dishes, countertops, and utensils with hot soapy water.
- Never place cooked food back on a plate that previously held raw meat, poultry, seafood, or eggs.

Cold Storage Chart

Item	Refrigerator at 40°F
Eggs, fresh in shell	3 to 5 weeks
Eggs, raw yolks, whites	2 to 4 days
Eggs, hard cooked	1 week
Salads – egg, chicken, ham, tuna	3 to 5 days
Luncheon meats	3 to 5 days
Bacon	7 days
Hamburger & stew meat	1 to 2 days
Ground turkey, veal, pork, lamb	1 to 2 days
Fresh beef, veal, lamb, pork	
Steaks	3 to 5 days
Chops	3 to 5 days
Roast	3 to 5 days
Soups & Stews	3 to 4 days
Cooked meat and meat casseroles	3 to 4 days
Fresh poultry	
Chicken or turkey – whole	1 to 2 days
Chicken or turkey – pieces	1 to 2 days
Cooked poultry	3 to 4 days
Pizza	3 to 4 days
Juices	
Unopened	3 weeks
Opened	7 to 10 days
Butter	1 to 3 months
Cheese—hard (cheddar, swiss)	
Unopened	6 months
Opened	3 to 4 weeks
Cheese - soft	1 week
Cream cheese	2 weeks
Milk	1 week
Sour cream	7 to 21 days
Yogurt	7 to 14 days
Fish, uncooked	1 to 2 days
Fish, cooked	3 to 4 days

- To prevent juices from raw meat, poultry, or seafood from dripping onto other foods in the refrigerator, put these foods in a sealed container or bag and place on the bottom shelf of your refrigerator.
- Sauce that is used to marinate raw meat, poultry or seafood should not be used on cooked food unless it is boiled first.

Wash all produce under running water before cutting, cooking, or eating so that dirt and bacteria are not transferred from the fruit or vegetable onto the knife. Firm produce such as potatoes, melon, and cucumbers should be scrubbed with a clean vegetable brush under running water and then dried with a clean towel before cutting.

Manufacturers will sometimes stamp a "**sell by**" date on a package. This date is intended for the retailer only and it indicates when an item should be removed from a shelf. This stamp is usually found on perishable items such as dairy and meat. Before purchasing an item, check to make sure this date has not passed.

Some of the other stamps used by manufacturers are: "**best by**", "**best before**", "**use by**", or "**best if used by**". These dates are intended for the consumer and indicate the date when an item should be used by for the best taste and quality. Check to make sure this date has not passed before purchasing.

Most pantry items can be stored in their original packaging, with the exception of sugar, flour, corn meal, rice, and grains. These items should be transferred to airtight containers as soon as you open them and used within the suggested timeframe. Follow the manufacturers "use by" date and check the packaging for any additional information about storage and shelf life once the package is opened.

Pantry Storage Chart

Item	Unopened	Opened
Cereal	6 – 12 months	3 months
Coffee beans (vacuum sealed)	3-4 months	1-2 weeks
Ground (vacuum sealed)	3 months	1 week
Flour (white)	1 year	1 year
Sugar – granulated (if stored in an airtight container kept cool and dry)	indefinitely	indefinitely
Honey	1 year	1 year
Rice	2 years	1 year
Pasta (dried)	2 years	2 years
Beans – dried	2 years	2 years
Oats	6 months	6 months
Chips & pretzels	3 months	2 weeks
Crackers	3 months	2 weeks
Granola bars	3 months	2 weeks
Dried fruit	6 months	1 month
Peanut butter	9 months	3 months
Spices	2 years	1 year
Vinegars	2 years	1 year
Oils (Olive, Vegetable, & Corn)	1 year	6 months

The following pantry items require refrigeration once opened:

Item	Unopened	Opened
Broths (canned or boxed)	2 years	4 days
Jams/jelly	1 year	6 months
Maple syrup	2 years	1 year
Mustard	1 year	1 year
Ketchup	1 year	6 months
Mayonnaise	3 months	2 months
Salad dressing	1 year	1 month
Nut oils: sesame walnut,etc.	1 year	6 months
Barbecue sauce	1 year	4 months
Salsa (jarred)	1 year	1 month

Most canned good will last between 2–5 years with the exception of high-acid foods such as tomatoes and citrus fruit. They will keep for approximately 18 months. When purchasing canned goods always check the expiration date and avoid dented or damaged cans (they can be contaminated). Canned goods should be kept in a cool dark place, such as a cabinet or pantry. Never store them near a heat source or in a damp place; temperature fluctuations will cause the contents to break down faster.

Storage Tips for Fresh Produce

Once home, refrigerate any produce that was purchased pre-cut or peeled. Perishable fruits and vegetables should be stored in the refrigerator. Follow the recommended "use by" date on pre-packaged salad greens. Eating them past their expiration date can cause sickness from bacterial spoilage.

Potatoes and onions should be stored separately in a cool dark place. Onions, garlic, and shallots can be stored together in a well-ventilated container, such as a basket.

Keep most fruit out at room temperature to ripen and refrigerate before serving if you prefer to eat it cold.

Is frozen food safe? According to the USDA Food Safety and Inspection Service, food stored constantly at 0°F will always be safe. Freezing preserves food because it prevents the growth of microorganisms that cause food spoilage and food-borne illness. The freezer storage recommendations in the table on the following page are for quality purposes only—foods eaten within these timeframes will retain more of their delicious original taste.

You can freeze meat and poultry in its supermarket package. If you plan on storing the food longer than a month or two you should over-wrap the package in foil or plastic wrap, or place it in a freezer bag. And don't forget to label and date packages before putting them in the freezer!

Properly storing your food will help maintain quality and prevent "freezer burn," which is caused by air reaching the surface of the food. Freezer burn is not harmful to your food, but it can detract from its taste and appearance, so make sure all your freezer packaging is airtight. If you have items in your freezer that are covered with "freezer burn" I would suggest tossing them because the quality of the items is likely to be poor.

Freezer Storage Chart (0° F)

Item	Months
Bacon and Sausage	1 to 2
Bagels	3
Bread	3
Butter	6
Casseroles	2 to 3
Cheeses (block) Hard	6
Cheese (grated)	4
Egg Whites or egg substitutes	12
Fish (non-fatty)	6
Frozen Dinners and Entrees	3 to 4
Gravy (meat or poultry)	2 to 3
Ham, hot dogs, and lunchmeats	1 to 2
Meat, uncooked roasts	4 to 12
Meat, uncooked steaks or chops	4 to 12
Meat, uncooked ground	3 to 4
Meat, cooked	2 to 3
Milk	3
Nuts (shelled)	6
Poultry, uncooked whole	12
Poultry, uncooked parts	9
Poultry, cooked	4
Shrimp	6
Soups and stews	2 to 3
Yogurt	2

My final advice to you is to become comfortable preparing meals in your kitchen. When you prepare more of your meals, you save money. When you control the ingredients used to make your meals, you eat in a healthier fashion. I encourage you to experiment with your cooking.

My son, John, loves to try new recipes. Ask friends for their favorite recipes. Invite them over to test the recipe in your kitchen. Maybe you will like the outcome, maybe you won't, but you will have fun in the preparation!

I hope you derive as much pleasure from cooking as I do.

- Joan Norfleet

"The art of living easily as to money is to pitch your scale of living one degree below your means."

Sir Henry Thomas, Police Magistrate
1807–1876

Chapter

Organizing Your Budget

I think almost all of us would agree that operating within a budget and being financially responsible are goals that are worth the effort it takes to achieve them. Having too much debt and worrying about how to pay the bills produces lots of stress and anxiety. One of the best ways to avoid that stress is to get in the habit of using and working with a budget. But what is a budget?

A budget is essentially a plan that takes into account your financial resources and your expenditures and makes sure that your expenditures don't exceed your resources. It's as simple as that. The trick is to have a plan that works for you.

Take the time to figure out exactly how much money you have coming in, exactly what your expenses are, and how much you typically spend on non-essential items—those are the things you want but don't need to have in order to live comfortably. This chapter will take you, step by step, through the process of organizing a budget, and it will give you strategies that will help keep you on track.

Numbers, Numbers ... Who's Got The Numbers?

Where do you find the numbers to work with when you create a budget? Start by keeping track of all your non-fixed expenses for two weeks. Rent, utilities, insurance, and car and student loans are generally predictable expenses. Non-fixed items such as groceries, coffee, meals, or bar tabs vary each time.

Carry a little notebook and pen with you at all times. Every time you pay for something, make a note of the amount spent and what you spent it on. You'll be surprised by how many small transactions you make in a day. At the end of the two weeks, go through your notebook and divide your expenditures into categories.

The table below shows some sample categories for non-fixed items. I recommend that you don't use "Miscellaneous" as a category. That term can describe almost anything and will make budgeting more difficult. Try to be reasonably specific.

Sample Non-Fixed Categories
- Restaurant/ meals out
- Coffee/snacks
- Groceries
- Entertainment/fun
- Bar receipts
- Gas
- Clothes
- Hair/ grooming
- Drugstore/toiletries
- Personal Items

After tracking your expenses for a couple weeks, you should have a pretty good idea of how much you generally spend on things like groceries, gas, eating out, entertainment, and personal items. Once you have those numbers, go back and take a good hard look at them. Ask yourself if you are spending your money wisely. Did you have very little money left at the end of the month? Were you counting the days until your bank account was replenished, either with a paycheck, alimony, or an allowance?

If these questions make you pause, then you should probably cut back on some of the expenses. Maybe you can save money by bringing your lunch to work. Perhaps you can save money on gas for your car by planning your errand route so that you take care of the errands in batches instead of making multiple trips. My son Andy is a really nice and caring person—he is also a very soft touch. His friends like to call and ask him to come pick them up so they can do things like go to the beach together.

That sounds really friendly, but the end result is that he is buying the gas for his car and doing the extra driving to pick his friends up and then take them home again. He has learned—although it is hard for him—to ask his friends to chip in for gas money so that he is not the only one paying out of pocket.

How To Use The Numbers In Your Budget

Now that you know what your categories are, think about how much money you can afford to allocate to each category. Fixed expenses are easier to predict. For instance, your rent is the same every month and is due on the first of the month. Your car loan is a monthly fixed amount, as is your education loan.

You may have other expenses like car insurance, where your premium is annual, or semi-annual, rather than monthly. In cases like that, you'll need to figure out the monthly cost to plan your budget. For example, let's say that your car insurance premium is $720 and it is due every six months. To find the amount you need to save every month to pay this bill just divide the total premium by 6:

$720/6 = $120

So you need to set aside $120 from your income each month to put toward your car insurance premium. If you have an expense that is paid annually, you would divide by 12 instead of 6. For instance, let's say that you've taken out a renter's insurance policy on the belongings in your apartment, and the annual premium is $480. To figure out the monthly charge:

$480/12 = $40

That's another $40 you need to add into your budget calculations.

If you work for a company and the benefits include health, dental, and life insurance, these expenses will be deducted from the salary you receive. If you work for a small company, you may be seeking your own individual policies and paying these insurance costs yourself. In that case, you'll need to expense your costs over time as indicated in the previous examples.

Cutting Costs

Your electricity bill may fluctuate depending on the time of the
year, the amount of natural light your apartment gets, and how
you set your thermostat. You can save some money on electricity
if you remember to switch off the lights when you are not in the
room and by keeping a close eye on your thermostat. If you have
a thermostat that you can program, you can set it to raise and
lower the temperature automatically at specific times each day.
I am not suggesting that you turn your apartment into an icebox
or a sauna! I am, however, advocating that you not keep the
apartment as comfortable during the day when you are not home
as you would when you are home. In cold months, program
the thermostat to begin heating your home to a comfortable
temperature around the time you generally return from work.
You can also program the thermostat to lower the temperature
slightly at night.

My advice for the summer months is exactly the opposite—don't
waste energy cooling the apartment during the day when you're
not home, and let the temperature get a little higher at night when
you sleep.

Another way to reduce your use of electricity is by unplugging
the appliances that you are not actively using. Some appliances
draw electricity when they are plugged into an outlet, even if
they aren't turned on.

Your phone bill may fluctuate depending on your plan and how
you use your phone. Andy does a lot of text messaging, and he
used to exceed his monthly text message allotment all the time,

which led to some very expensive phone bills! By investigating the different plans offered by his phone company, he found out that he could have unlimited text messages by paying a slightly higher base rate each month. That really works well for him, because now he can text all he wants without worrying about extra charges.

Recently, our other son, Alex, moved from a lovely apartment in Jacksonville, Florida to New York City because of a job transfer. Alex had a large apartment in Jacksonville, complete with washer and dryer, and we thought he would never be able to afford an equally nice apartment in New York City.

Alex was thrilled with the prospect of moving to New York and told us not to worry; he would find an apartment and also find a roommate to share expenses. We were a little concerned. How was he going to do all that from Jacksonville? We knew the company Alex works for was not going to pay his airfare to New York and give him time off from work to go apartment hunting.

This is what he did: Alex networked through his friends from college and graduate school. He found that one of his friends knew a guy named Harry in New York City whose roommate was moving out. Harry had actually gone to the same university as Alex, so they were somewhat acquainted. Alex's friend put him in touch with Harry, and they decided that Alex would replace the outgoing roommate. They figured out together what furniture Alex should bring with him from his Jacksonville apartment. Now Alex has a nice affordable apartment since he is able to share the living expenses with Harry.

Money Saving Tips!
- Compare cell phone plans
- Carpool
- Prioritize your errands
- Get basic cable or satellite TV
- Program your thermostat
- Unplug appliances when not in use
- Find a roommate and share living
  expenses

Now let's put it all together.
1. Use the sample budget worksheet below as a guideline.
2. Fill out the top portion of the blank budget worksheet with your expenses that are paid monthly.
3. Look back at your daily expenses notebook.
4. Make a good estimate of your weekly expenses.
5. Fill in your weekly expenses on the bottom portion of the budget worksheet.

Sample Monthly Budget Worksheet

Monthly Expenses	Amount Paid
Rent	$700
Electric	$30
Telephone	$50
Car Loan	$150
Car Insurance	$60
Education Loan	$75
Water	$10
Garbage	$5
Internet	$25
TV	$30
Renter's Insurance	$70
(paid quarterly; $210/3=$70)	
Total Monthly Expenses:	$1,145

Weekly Expenses	Amount Paid
Groceries	$80
Restaurant	$50
Take-Out	$60
Lunch	$30
Personal Expenses (manicure/pedicure)	$15
Haircut	$20
Clothes	$20
Dry Cleaning	$10
Laundry	$15
Public Transportation	$10
Total Weekly Expenses:	$310

Monthly Budget Worksheet

Monthly Expenses	Amount Paid
Rent	_____
Electric	_____
Telephone	_____
Car Loan	_____
Car Insurance	_____
Education Loan	_____
Water	_____
Garbage	_____
Internet	_____
TV	_____
Renter's Insurance	_____
Total Expenses:	

Weekly Expenses	Amount Paid
Groceries	_____
Restaurant	_____
Take-Out	_____
Lunch	_____
Personal Expenses (manicure/pedicure)	_____
Haircut	_____
Clothes	_____
Dry Cleaning	_____
Laundry	_____
Public Transportation	_____
Total weekly expenses:	

Please remember that your budget will change as you and your circumstances change. For instance, if you change jobs and receive a larger salary, you may want to put more money aside to save. Maybe you have a family and have expenses related to your spouse and children. Take some time every year to re-evaluate your budget and amend it to fit your current situation.

Credit Cards, Debit Cards, and Hidden Fees

Credit Cards: Use Them Wisely
Two important items I left off of the budget worksheet are credit card bills and automatic deductions from your bank account (for things like online bill paying fees, other banking fees, and online music or movie subscriptions).

Credit cards can be very useful when they are used sparingly. They become a problem when you rely on them as your primary means of paying for life's everyday expenses. Then the amount billed on the card can easily become more than you can afford to pay in a single month. Consequently, you end up paying the purchase price of your items plus interest.

Think about it this way: When you use a credit card you are essentially "renting money" from the credit card company. This company charges you a fee—interest—every time the amount on the card is not paid in full. The higher the balance on the card, the more "rent" the company charges.

My advice is to try and keep your use of a credit card to a minimum. Most of the time you should limit credit card use to urgent situations when using credit is a necessity: If your car needs new brakes or tires; if there is a family emergency and you need to fly home; if your computer's hard drive crashes beyond recovery. I am sure you can think of other examples.

The point is that the credit cards should not be used recklessly. I understand the promise of airline miles and free gifts using "Reward Points" can be very alluring, but these do not make up for the huge cost of the interest payments. In order to gather enough reward points to buy anything, you have to spend a lot of money. Please keep that in mind.

Save for a Rainy Day

You've heard the expression "to save for a rainy day." It is defined by the *Cambridge Dictionary of American Idioms* to mean "to keep something, especially money, for a time in the future when it might be needed."

It is really critical that you get into the habit of saving as much money as you can. Not only are you saving for your future, you are also saving money because you never know when that rainy day is coming and you might need a little extra money.

For instance, your computer may crash and you'll need to pay for emergency repairs, your car might break down, or you may accidently drop your cell phone and watch it break into smithereens. These would be necessary but unexpected (and not budgeted) expenses. In my book, that would be just cause to use your "rainy day" money.

Where does this "rainy day" money come from? Nick's rule of thumb, and something we have encouraged Alex and Andy to do, is to save 10% of your monthly income, if possible.

The habit of putting something—even if it is only your pocket change to begin with—in a savings account where it will earn interest and you cannot easily access it is a critical habit to form. The banks in your neighborhood all have savings account plans. Take a look at a few banks and compare the interest rates and minimum balances. Also make sure you look online. Some financial institutions offer online-only savings accounts. Look at www.money-rates.com/savings.htm to compare rates and see which financial institution best fits your needs.

You should use a credit card to pay for those necessary-but-unexpected expenses that aren't included in your budget. You can then tap into the "rainy day" money in your savings account to help pay the credit card bill. This will let you pay off the entire amount faster, reducing the amount of interest that accrues.

If you can put aside more than pocket change, you should look into a 401k plan if your employer offers one. Find out how much of your monthly contribution your employer will match, then make sure you contribute at least that much.

For example, if your employer will match your contribution to the 401k plan provided that you contribute 5% of your monthly gross then you should contribute at least 5% every month in order to get the matched amount from your employer. If you can contribute 8% or even 10% your employer will still only contribute 5%, but just imagine how quickly your savings will grow! You can find a good article that will tell you all about 401k plans at the website money.howstuffworks.com/personal-finance/retirement-planning/401k.htm .

Another way to save money is to invest in a CD (certificate of deposit) at your bank. Banks will let you buy a CD for a fixed period of time, usually with a minimum of 3 months. The longer you keep your money in a CD, the more interest you will earn. Be advised, though, that you will not be able to use this money while it is invested in the CD. Take a look at the website: www.cdrates.bankaholic.com. This site compares the rates and minimum deposits at many financial institutions.

Remember, you are saving money for future needs and expenses. You should not be looking for instant huge growth in your savings account, but as long as you set that money aside and don't touch it, it will grow. Make putting money aside something you do conscientiously and regularly. This is a good habit to cultivate.

You might want to schedule making a deposit to your savings account on your calendar. Put it as a regular task on your "to do" list. Before long, saving will become part of your regular routine! If you are lucky enough to receive a cash bonus or monetary gifts for birthday, Christmas, or Chanukah, you should consider putting some of it into your savings account. Another thing to consider is investing some of your money in mutual funds or an IRA. You will have it later—maybe ten, twenty, or even thirty years later—for big budget items or even your own retirement. Here is a website to review for great information on investing. This site features articles on how and where to invest your money for steady growth: www.money.cnn. com/pf/.

Carrying Cash

Want to save even more money? Pay for things with cash whenever possible. I know it can be really inconvenient to make a trip to the bank and withdraw the amount of cash you have allocated for the week. Credit and debit cards are so much easier to carry. They take up less space. They are fast; all you do is swipe and go. For some cards, you can just tap the reader, and you don't even have to enter a pin number or sign your name. Here is the catch: you can easily lose track of how much you have spent.

Now picture this: You have withdrawn $210 to spend on groceries for the week, budgeting $30 per day. You have to make this amount last 7 whole days, and as the days go by you can watch that pile of money get smaller. Let's say you're are in the grocery store and you see a few items on sale that you would like to have but that you don't need (perhaps candy or beer). Because you are paying cold, hard cash, it will be easy for you to see that if you buy those sale items, you won't have enough money for the things you really need. It helps you limit your impulse buying.

To take this concept one step further; let's say you have budgeted $210 for groceries, $20 for personal items, $40 for gas, and $50 for entertainment for the week. You withdraw a total of $320 from the bank on Friday. Put $210 in an envelope labeled "Groceries"; put $20 in another envelope labeled "Personal Items'"; put another $40 in a third envelope labeled "Gas"; and put the remaining $50 in an envelope labeled "Fun Money." As you plan your day, only put into your wallet the money you plan to spend that day.

For example, if you are going to the movies Saturday afternoon with your friends, then that morning you will withdraw $10 from your "Fun Money" envelope, and you may take a few more dollars from that envelope just in case you decide to go somewhere for a bite to eat after the movies. Managing your money this way has two important benefits. First of all, you are limiting your impulse spending. Secondly, paying with cash makes it easier to stick to your budget.

When you use a credit card, it is altogether too easy to spend a little more (or a lot more) than you really should. Rationalizing the expense could go something like this: "I know I shouldn't be buying this, I really don't need it, but I really want it. I promise to spend less next month to make up for this." Carrying cash makes you think twice because you have to physically take the money out of your wallet and put it on the counter. You either have enough money with you or you don't. The added benefit of using cash is that you never have to worry about paying interest on your purchases.

"We can lick gravity, but sometimes the paperwork is overwhelming."

Wernher von Braun, Scientist
1912–1977

Chapter

Organizing Your Papers

The amount of mail that comes into our homes is mind-boggling. According to the United States Postal Service, the amount of bulk mail delivered annually is about 17.8 tons or the weight of 4 elephants. Did you know that on average each of us receives as much mail in a month as our grandparents did in a year? Individually we spend about 34 hours a year opening unwanted mail. Credit card companies send us countless solicitations. Catalogs flood our mailboxes—particularly around the holidays. And then there are bills, statements, solicitations for charitable donations, and sometimes an invitation or two. If you have friends who still write "snail mail" letters you may even receive a correspondence. So, what can you do to stay in control of the influx of paper?

I met Ned and June a few years ago when all the incoming mail was turning their kitchen counter into a choppy sea of paper piles. They were newlyweds. Ned had just begun law school, and June was working as a social worker. Their time at home together was limited, and they did not want to spend the majority of it searching for documents or trying to figure out if bills were lurking in the piles of paper. This was a major frustration for them. Ned did not want to miss vital information pertaining to his classes, and neither of them wanted to be delinquent with a bill. They were just beginning their life together and did not want to jeopardize their credit rating because of a late payment. They asked me to help them find a good solution to their problem.

Good Habits and Routines

I learned that the routine they followed was to pick up the mail at the end of the day and plop it on the counter. Sometimes it would be a week or more before they would even look at the mail that had come into their home. I told them this habit of ignoring the mail had to change. I asked Ned to talk to me about the different types of mail they receive. We determined that some of the mail could be dropped directly into the recycling bin or shredded—things like fliers, unwanted catalogues, advertisements, and solicitations that they know hold no interest. Other mail like catalogs and magazines, which they are sure they will read, could be placed in a basket near their couch. The remaining mail, consisting mostly of bills, statements, and invitations, would be opened and sorted into broad categories right away.

Mail Sorting System

I had brought with me a small freestanding hanging file holder. I also had some hanging files, manila folders, and plastic tabs. I labeled the manila files and the plastic tabs for the hanging folders: "Bills To Pay," "Important Information for June," "Important Information For Ned," "Events To Consider," "Tax Related," and "Things To File."

We went through the paper bag of mail that June had collected from the kitchen counter. In a short period of time the mail was sorted. Ned and June agreed that every day when the mail came into the house it would be sorted and the items would go into the folders, the magazine basket, the shredder, or the recycling bin. They also agreed that once a week they would go through the folders to pay bills, file statements, and make decisions about the invitations. This solution cleared up their kitchen counter and put them in control of the mail.

A few weeks later, I checked back with Ned and June to find out if they were having any trouble keeping up with the mail. Ned told me that at first both he and June had to be really disciplined.

They had to make a concerted effort every day to go through the mail, sort it, shred it, and file it appropriately in the free standing file holder. June decided to set aside about 15 minutes every Saturday morning to file the statements in the file cabinet while Ned paid any bills that were due.

As the days went on, they saw that the effort was paying off; the kitchen counter remained clear, and the bills and other papers were easy to find. It became easier and easier to follow through with the mail sorting process. Ned told me they no longer even thought about it—it had become part of their regular routine. I was thrilled for Ned and June! Changing a habit is never easy; when you change a habit, celebrate!

Use the self-assessment chart on the next page to see which of your mail sorting habits you may want to change.

Self-Assessment Chart

	Always	Almost Always	Rarely	Never
Put the mail in the same place in my home.				
Recycle unwanted catalogs & mail				
Open mail every day				
Sort mail every day				
Plan a time to file at least once a week				
Put anything tax related in the same place				

Make the System Work for You

If the influx of mail is a problem for you, you can follow the same strategy as Ned and June but modify it to fit your needs. You might decide to use different names for the files you keep at your fingertips. Label them any way that makes sense to you.

The important thing is that you know where to put the different types of mail so that when the time comes to reconcile your bank statement, pay a bill, or respond to an invitation, you know exactly where to look for it.

There are many different kinds of freestanding mail holders. Find one that fits the space you have available and that appeals to you. If you are a visually oriented person, you may not want to put your papers into a file folder. A better solution for you might be a multi-tiered paper sorter. You can label the outside edge of each tier, so you can see at a glance the kind of mail each slot holds. These mail holders can even be attractive and/or colorful.

If you do prefer to use file folders, you can color coordinate hanging files with the inserted folder if you want to. You can even have a color represent a particular category. Remember, these files should be broad in category and they (the files) are just a first response method for getting the papers sorted into major categories. Here are a few photos of some mail sorting devices.

1. Clear Hanging File Holder

2. Inclined Letter File Sorter

3. Multi-tiered Paper Sorter

4. Accordion File

Office supply stores and big merchandisers like Target and Walmart have a variety of desk and mail organizing items. You can also check out these websites for more ideas:

- www.containerstore.com
- www.onlineorganizing.com
- www.kangaroomstorage.com
- www.seejanework.com
- www.officecandy.com

Mail Sorting Tips

When you retrieve the mail from the mailbox, sort it right away. Open the statements and put them in the "To File" folder. Open the bills and put them in the "To Pay" folder. If an invitation arrives in the mail and you know you will definitely accept the invitation, take a minute or two and respond right away. Once you have responded make sure to put all the information in your calendar—either your electronic calendar, or a paper one.

Essential Tools for Handling Mail

1. Shredder
2. Place to put sorted mail
3. Folders
4. Envelopes
5. Stamps
6. Return address labels

If you are unsure of your response to the invitation, or you think there may be a conflict, put that piece of mail into a folder labeled "To Consider." The important thing is to open each piece of mail and put it in a temporary home—but only until you have time to properly deal with it. Make a date with yourself to attend to the mail once a week to pay bills, file statements, and respond to invitations. If it can be the same day each week, even better!

Some of your incoming mail is time sensitive—it has a due date associated with it. For example: bill payments might be due by the first of the month, the deadline to respond to an invitation could be next week, or the expiration date for a coupon may be in 10 days. Always deal with the time-sensitive mail first!

Mail Sorting Strategies

1. Sort through the mail every day.
2. Recycle any catalogues or fliers you KNOW (be honest) you will not ever look at.
3. Shred anything that has your personal or account information on it—especially anything that says "pre-approved."
4. Put the magazines you want to read in one place.
5. Open the bills and put them in a "To Pay" folder.
6. Open statements and put them in a place to be filed.
7. Make a date with yourself each week to pay bills and to file statements into a designated file.
8. Put invitations or events to attend in one place.

Which Papers to Keep and How to Find Them

How do you determine which papers are important to keep? Wouldn't it be nice if those documents came with a little post-it note attached that said something like "Keep me for 12 months" or "Keep me for 7 years?" Unfortunately, this is only a dream I have.

There are some papers and documents that you must keep, like the title for your car, financial records, high school diploma, tax returns, and health records. Some you keep only for a year, some indefinitely, some you keep for seven to ten years, and some you keep until a replacement document arrives. It is up to you to know what they are and how long you need to have them taking up space.

It is important to keep these papers in one place and in a way that you can find what you need the minute you want to. You can organize the files by category/topic or alphabetically.

On the next few pages is a sample filing system set up by category. I use a labeler to make labels to insert into the plastic tab and affix to the folder. You can manually print the labels with a pen, pencil, or even select a colored marker to represent a category. You can also print the labels on your computer. How you label is up to you! I recommend putting an identically labeled folder (manila or colored) inside the hanging file so that if you remove the inside folder you know exactly where to put it back.

Essential Tools for Filing
1. Interior folders, manila or colored
2. Hanging Files, regular and 2-inch box bottom (You can buy plain or colorful ones.)
3. Labels
4. Permanent marker
5. Plastic tabs
6. File cabinet (2-drawer) or 2 Filing boxes
7. Plastic bags that seal shuts

Sample Categorical Filing System:

Appliances
1. Blender
2. Microwave
3. Washing machine
4. Vacuum cleaner

Attach the receipt to the user manual for each appliance. Often the warranty information is on the receipt, particularly if you purchased an extended warranty. Rewrite the date of purchase and the expiration date of the warranty in pen as this information will fade over time. Keep the manual in the folder along with any maintenance or repair receipts.

Car
❏ Purchase or lease agreement
❏ Maintenance records
❏ Title (copy)
❏ Registration (copy)

Keep maintenance records to verify the service that has been done to the car; you may need this information if you sell it. Keep the originals of the documents in a safe deposit box at your bank.

Education
❏ Diplomas, certificates (copies)
❏ Tuition (Keep the signed tuition agreement in this file)
  Keep the originals of the documents in a safe deposit box at your bank.

Electronics
❏ Camera
❏ Cell Phone
❏ Cell Phone Service Provider Contract
❏ Computer
❏ Printer
❏ TV

Attach the receipt to the manual for each electronic device. Rewrite the date of purchase in pen. As with appliances, the warranty expiration date is often on the receipt—rewrite that in pen also. Receipts can fade over time. Keep the manual in the folder for the device.

Put any extra cords or hardware in a plastic baggie that seals shut. Write the name of the device they came with on the bag with a permanent marker. Keep the bag in the hanging folder.

NOTE: It is best to use the 2-inch box-bottom hanging folders for files that have software manuals and extra hardware or cords.

Employment
☐ Employee Handbook/ Policies
☐ Record of past employment and W-2 forms
☐ Resume (Keep an electronic copy and a paper copy in the file)

Finances
Keep the current year in the easy-to-access file, and keep at least 7–10 years of financial records in total. You can archive previous years with your past tax returns in a separate file drawer or a file box.
☐ Checking account
☐ Savings account
☐ Safe deposit box information and inventory of contents
☐ Credit card(s)—keep the agreement showing your interest rate and the privacy policy in this file
☐ Investment accounts (bonds, stocks, IRA)—keep indefinitely
☐ Mortgage
☐ Educational loan
☐ FAFSA
☐ Car Loan

House
- ❏ Household furnishings inventory (Keep one disc in the folder, and put a duplicate disc in the safe deposit box at the bank. See Chapter 3 for more information about the household inventory.)
- ❏ List of any reliable technicians or repairmen for your home with their phone numbers
- ❏ Receipts for any furniture and furnishings

Insurance
- ❏ Car insurance
- ❏ Health insurance
- ❏ Renter's insurance
- ❏ Home owner's insurance
- ❏ Insurance riders
- ❏ Life Insurance
- ❏ Disability Insurance

Medical Records
- ❏ Doctor's names/addresses/phone numbers
- ❏ Immunization records
- ❏ Rehab (physical therapy or alcohol/drug) records
- ❏ Hospitalization records

Safe Deposit Box
Keep all original documents in a safe deposit box at your bank. If there were ever a question of your identity, these original documents would prove your claim beyond a shadow of a doubt. Also, if there was a natural disaster that destroyed your home filing system these records would be safe.

Keep a current list of the documents at the bank in the Safe Deposit Box File. It should include such items as:

Baptismal record	Birth certificate
Car title	Certificates and diplomas
Deed to your house	Divorce records
Household inventory disc	Marriage license
Passport	Social Security card
Will	

Social Security
❑ Social security no longer sends a paper statement. Keep a copy of your Social Security card in your Vital Documents file and keep the original in your safe deposit box.

Tax-Related Information
❑ Keep the current year information in an easy-to-access file
❑ Income
❑ Charitable donation receipts (Goodwill, monetary donations, etc.)
❑ Receipts for deductible business or personal expenses
❑ Year end financial statements

Tax Returns
Keep income tax returns for at least 7–10 years. Archive them in a box or separate file drawer with all your past financial statements. Check with a tax accountant before shredding any of these archived documents.

Vital Documents
- ❒ Adoption papers (copy)
- ❒ Baptismal records (copy)
- ❒ Birth certificate (copy)
- ❒ Business Ownership papers (copy)
- ❒ Child custody agreements (copy)
- ❒ Citizenship & Naturalization papers (copy)
- ❒ Death Certificate (copy)
- ❒ Deed to your home (copy)
- ❒ Divorce records (copy)
- ❒ Domestic Partnership agreements (copy)
- ❒ Durable Power of Attorney (copy)
- ❒ End of Life plans—include funeral service, burial or cremation, and perpetual care contract (copy)
- ❒ Living Will (copy)
- ❒ Login user name & password information for all financial files
- ❒ Marriage license (copy)
- ❒ Military Discharge papers (copy)
- ❒ Passport (copy of the inside page)
- ❒ Social Security card (copy)
- ❒ Veterinary records (copy)
- ❒ Will (copy)

Keep a scanned copy of all these documents on a jump drive that you can take with you in case of a natural disaster or emergency. Keep the originals in your safe deposit box.

Once you have determined the filing method that will work for you, you need to have a place to put the files. If you have the space, a two-drawer filing cabinet is perfect. If you do not, office supply stores have lots of alternatives to filing cabinets, like a file box (cardboard or plastic) or a file cart (which can sometimes be wheeled into a closet or under a table and hidden).

Remember that what you keep in your files changes as your needs change. You can add or remove files and make new categories. Plan some time in early January to make the current year folders for your financial and tax files. Go through all the current files to make sure you are only keeping the information you need. Recycle or shred any documents that are no longer pertinent. These actions will keep your file drawers from becoming overloaded with outdated documents.

Organizing Receipts

There are a few different kinds of receipts. There are the receipts that are attached to the bottom of your monthly bills, and there are also transaction receipts. The monthly receipts serve to verify that you have paid the bill. I advise my clients to write the date paid and the check number on the portion of the statement that you keep. There are several different options as to how to deal with these monthly receipts. You can keep them month to month, shredding the previous month. Another option is to keep the receipts for as many months as you want, up to one year.

If you receive and pay the bill electronically, you can print a hard copy of the statement and write the confirmation number on the paper statement. Or you can print the statement into a PDF file, making a note of the confirmation number. Create a folder in your computer for the PDFs. That folder could be labeled "paid bills; month & year" or any other such label that will help you remember where to file these statements!

Remember to shred the paper statements when you are ready to discard them!

How to File Monthly Receipts

1. Use a pre-labeled accordion file. File the paid receipts by month. Keep the accordion file somewhere handy,
OR
2. Make 12 hanging files and folders and label them, one for each month.
3. Keep the hanging files in the front of the top drawer of your filing cabinet with the current month first.
4. Put the monthly receipts of bills in the folder.
5. Keep these receipts for 12 months.
OR
6. Have 1 hanging file labeled 'Paid Bills' with 1 interior manila folder.
OR
7. Have a folder in your computer in which to save PDF copies of statements you pay electronically & scans of paid paper statements.

When you go to the store and make a transaction of any kind, you receive a receipt. It doesn't matter if you are paying cash, using a check, or using a credit or debit card. You even get a receipt for making a deposit or withdrawal at an ATM machine. What should you do with the receipt? Do you throw it out and hope you remember to enter it into some sort of transaction or budget record? Do you toss it into a drawer? Do you file it in the back of your wallet until your wallet becomes so full that you empty all those bits of paper into the recycling bin? Perhaps the receipts go into your pocket. These little bits of paper are a nuisance to keep track of.

Just as the mail should be dealt with every day, so should these little transaction records. Each time you get a receipt, take a moment at the cash register to make a note on it, if you need to. Some receipts are self-explanatory. For instance, the receipt you get at the grocery store will have the name of the store and all the grocery items listed. It will also indicate if you paid with cash or a credit card.

However, if you went to a department store and bought a pair of jeans the receipt may simply have printed on it the item number and the name of the department—Men's Wear, for example. It would be helpful to put the name of the item in small print at the top of your receipt (for example, "jeans").

It is also useful to write down if you used your debit or credit card. Make sure to get a receipt every time you go to the ATM machine to withdraw cash. Make a note on the receipt like "cash for the week" or "cash for dinner." These little notes to yourself will serve to jog your memory when you go to reconcile the receipts.

When you get home from shopping, after you have put your things away, take five minutes and go through your receipts. If you have the time, enter any cash transactions right away in your checkbook or in your computer finance program. But if you do not have time to deal with the receipts right away, where should you put them? There are many possible solutions to that dilemma.

I have a small 4x6 index card box with dividers on my desk. The dividers are labeled. I have categories for deposit receipts for checking and savings, credit card transactions, and cash transactions. Some of my clients use the 4x6 card box method.

One client, Jennifer, has labeled the file dividers in the card box with the budgeting categories for her non-fixed expenses. When Jennifer returns home from shopping, she makes a few notes on her receipts and then files them in her card box. Once a week she goes through the box and enters the expenses into her budget spreadsheet. Jennifer also records whether she spent cash or used a credit card.

At the end of the month, when her bank and credit card statements arrive in the mail, Jennifer goes through her receipts and matches them with the entries on the statements. Then she shreds some receipts, such as ATM withdrawal receipts, deposit receipts, and grocery receipts.

Small 4x6 Card Box

Other clients like to keep their receipts in large heavy plastic envelopes with a zipper across the top. Most office supply stores stock these envelopes. Another of my clients, Bill, has one envelope for each month. I labeled the envelopes for Bill with the names of the months. He puts the transaction receipts and the statements in the envelopes, and he keeps them in a drawer of his desk with the current month at the front of the drawer.

At the end of the month he goes through the envelope and staples the business transaction receipts to his business credit card statement. If he has paid in cash, Bill records the amount in his budget spreadsheet. After twelve months, if he has not had to refer to any of the receipts in the envelope, Bill shreds the receipts.

Large Heavy Plastic Envelope

Of course, there are exceptions to every filing system. If you bought an appliance, an electronic device, a piece of furniture, or any other expensive item, I recommend keeping these receipts in a different manner.

Appliances and electronic devices are sold with manuals and sometimes extended warranties. The end date of the warranty is usually printed on the receipt. Staple the receipt to the manual. Write the date of purchase on the manual in ink as well as the expiration date of the warranty, whether extended or not.

I made reference to these receipts in the "Sample Categorical Filing System." It is best to have these receipts with the manuals in case the item breaks and needs repair. Then you will have the manufacturer's registration number, the purchase date and amount at your fingertips when you call for assistance. Having the receipt will verify your claim.

Electronic Bill Paying

Most bills can now be received and paid online. There are at least three different ways to go about this process. Your bank probably has an online bill paying service to which you can subscribe. It is likely they will charge a monthly subscription fee that is automatically deducted from your checking account. This is one of those hidden fees to which I referred in Chapter Five. Make sure to include the monthly subscription fee in your budget.

Alternately, you can go to the vendor's website and pay your bill. For example, you can pay your electric bill by going to the electric company's website and setting up your account to be paid online.

Benefits of Electronic Bill Paying

- Receive your bills online—reducing the amount of mail in your mailbox.
- Reduce the amount of paper waste.
- Pay online—save the cost of a stamp.
- Schedule the payment to be withdrawn from your account and paid on the same day.
- Save time.

There are also several online bill paying computer programs. The initial investment for the software is expensive but the benefits are many. With a program like Quicken or Microsoft Money, you can download the transactions from all your accounts with one click. These programs allow you to sort transactions to help with budgeting. They also maintain your checkbook register and allow for virtually automatic account reconciliation.

Whichever method you choose—online bill paying through your personal bank, through an online bill paying software system, or on the vendor's website—you must keep track of your expenditures as though you were physically writing a check.

3 Ways to Pay

1. Sign up for online bill paying with your bank.
2. Use a money management software program.
3. Pay online through the vendor's website.

The bill paying automation can seem like magic! With one or two clicks of your mouse the bill is paid and the money is withdrawn from your account. You don't need to worry about writing the account number on a check, placing the check in the envelope (with the receipt facing the correct direction so that the address shows through the window), then remembering to mail the payment early enough that it is received before the due date.

My client Megan decided to receive almost all of her bills and financial statements electronically. She was also paying most of her bills online. Megan forgot that it was up to her to check the bills and statements for accuracy when they arrived in her email. After some time had passed, Megan noticed that one of her bank accounts seemed to have less money in it than it should.

She had forgotten that even though the paper statements were not cluttering up her desk, they still had to be looked over and reconciled every month. Megan had created a file where she saved the statements, so we went through them line by line. It turned out the bank had made a mistake. She had signed up for a service for a small fee and was being charged a different larger fee. Thankfully, Megan was able to get the charges reversed.

Automatic Deductions

Automatic deductions used to take me by surprise. I would see the amount of the deduction on my online bank statement and wonder "When did I spend that money?" The amount was the same as the monthly fee for Quicken, Check Free, or an online music download service. So I set an automatic reminder of my own in my online calendar a few days in advance of each deduction to indicate the amount that will be withdrawn from my checking account. Now, I am prepared to see the automatic deductions on my statement. That method might work for you, too!

How to File Electronic Receipts

Perhaps you have now decided to go ahead and pay most of your bills electronically. You may be wondering what to do if there is a problem with the vendor receiving payment. How do you verify that you actually sent a payment?

When you make an electronic payment, the vendor or your bank issues you a confirmation number. You can print a paper copy of the payment with confirmation number and file it with your other receipts, or you can save the payment receipt on your computer. If you use money management software like Quicken or Microsoft Money, you can record the confirmation number in the memo section of the transaction entry in the checkbook register. If you do not use such a program, save the e-mail confirmation the vendor sends you in an online payments mailbox. You can create a mailbox for different kinds of receipts. For instance, you could set up mailboxes labeled "Gifts purchased and sent online" or Bills paid by the month."

What to Shred

There are a few paper-related things that you can recycle or shred without even thinking about them. Warranty cards that come in the box with an appliance can usually be recycled. As I indicated before, warranties are now often generated at the time of purchase. They either show up on the cash register receipt or are included as a separate piece of paper with the sales receipt.

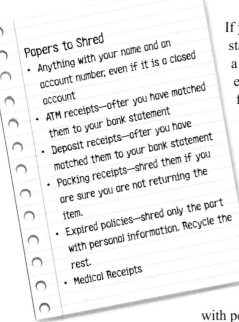

Papers to Shred
- Anything with your name and an account number, even if it is a closed account
- ATM receipts—after you have matched them to your bank statement
- Deposit receipts—after you have matched them to your bank statement
- Packing receipts—shred them if you are sure you are not returning the item.
- Expired policies—shred only the part with personal information. Recycle the rest.
- Medical Receipts

If you receive a paper bank statement there is usually a page that appears to be extra. Check it carefully for personal information. If there is an account number on it, shred it. When the new insurance policy arrives, the old one needs to leave the file and be shredded. This keeps your files from becoming full of outdated and irrelevant information. Always shred any document with personal information and/or account numbers. Identity theft is a scary proposition and anything you can do to prevent your identity from being stolen is worthwhile.

Here is a link to an online resource about identity theft:
http://www.justice.gov/criminal/fraud/websites/idtheft.html

"Time is the coin of your life. It is the only coin you have, and only you can determine how it will be spent. Be careful lest you let other people spend it for you."

Carl Sandberg, Poet
1878–1967

Chapter

Organize Your Time

Much of life is defined by time. No matter how much we want to take a break, we can't say "Stop the clock!" Time marches on. Some people have an innate sense of time. They are always aware of the clock. These people know how much time to allocate to a chore; they are in control. Others have trouble sensing the passage of time. These people always seem to be rushing off in a hurry because they are late or out of time. No matter which category you fall into, organizing your time well is a valuable skill to cultivate.

Many common expressions revolve around time. I'm sure that you can think of at least a few without even trying. Here are some of my favorites: "There's no time like the present," "Time flies when you're having fun," and "Invest your time wisely."

I particularly like these expressions because they ring true for me. I prefer to take care of chores when I have the time rather than put them off. I like being able to scratch them off my "To-Do" list. Hours can pass by in what seems like minutes when I am having fun, but minutes seem like hours when I am not.

Have you noticed that some financial terms are used when referring to time? If you are good at budgeting your time, you spend only the amount of time necessary on a task; you don't waste time. If you invest your time wisely, you have a great outcome—the project is successful. Just like money, time is precious and the challenge is that there are only 24 hours in a day. There are certain things that we have to do during those 24 hours, and there are other things we want to do each day. It is a balancing act. A survey done by FedEx Office in 2008 showed that 58% of people polled between the ages of 18–34 said a better work/life balance is very important to them. Organizing your time is the key to achieving this balance.

Time Management Basics

Life is simple when your time is well organized. Reflect back on what it was like when you were young—you were often told where to go and when to be there. For instance, you probably had to get up at a certain time in order to get to school before the first bell. I bet your mother or father reminded you to set your alarm clock at night, or maybe they even woke you up in the morning. Perhaps they made sure you had breakfast and were out the door in time to catch the bus. If you had after-school activities or appointments, you were told what they were and when to be there. You did not have to think about how you spent your time—it was taken care of for you. Looking back, that made life easier in some ways, didn't it?

Until recent times, life was simpler; work and leisure hours were more clearly defined. Most people had fixed schedules, with work on certain days for a certain number of hours. They did their job during these hours and they didn't take work home with them at night. Time spent at home was personal or family time only. Stores opened in the morning and closed at 5:00pm, and most stores were also closed on Sunday. Any shopping had to occur within that window. Our parents (or Grandparents) had to plan their time accordingly.

Now we can all be reached 24/7/365. Online stores are open whenever we feel like shopping, and we can access our bank accounts from home. Many people have flexible schedules that allow them to work during the day or at night. It is up to us, not the clock, to decide how much of our time to devote to work, to family, and to ourselves. We want to take the time available to us and use it to its best advantage. On the next few pages are strategies to learn and habits to cultivate that will help you find your own work/life balance.

Work/Life Balance Strategies

1. Create Daily Habits to Last a Lifetime
2. Make a "To-Do" List Everyday
3. Prioritize the Items on Your List
4. Plan Ahead
5. Set Goals
6. Use An Extra Calendar
7. Schedule Personal Time
8. Set Boundaries

Create Daily Habits to Last a Lifetime

My client Mary asked me why time simply races by when she gets dressed in the morning. I asked her what she meant. Mary explained that every morning she goes into her closet, chooses an outfit, and gets dressed. When she starts the process she notices the time, and then before she knows it half an hour has passed but it feels like only five minutes. Mary wanted me to explain how this could possibly happen.

Another client, Joe, had a similar story but it involved his computer. Joe told me that every morning he allows himself five minutes to sit down at his computer to check his emails, but in what seems like an instant, half an hour or more has passed. While these two clients have different stories, their dilemma is almost identical. They go to do a task and get so involved that they don't notice the passage of time, which is where we get the expression "Time stands still for no man." No matter what you are doing—or not doing—the clock still ticks.

The time Mary took to decide which outfit to wear made it impossible for her to complete the rest of her morning routine without being rushed. I advised Mary to take some time in the evening to look at her clothes and think about the next day's activities. If necessary, she could try on a few outfits and then decide which one to wear the following day, complete with all the accessories. Mary was not sure she liked the idea but she was willing to try it for a few days to see if this strategy would work. Every evening for a week Mary laid out her clothes for the next day. At the end of the week I called her to find out if her mornings were any easier.

Mary told me that at first she felt a little silly—a bit like a school girl choosing her outfit for the next day—but it did make mornings simpler. All she had to do was follow her routine, put on the previously selected outfit, and head out the door to work. Mary was very happy the guesswork had been removed. This strategy put more time into her morning routine, and this allowed her to have a stress free start to her day.

Joe and I looked over his morning routine. Joe works from home and likes to get his household chores out of the way before starting his work. These chores include walking the dog, doing a little gardening, and the daily cleaning and laundry. He had been trying to sneak in five minutes to take a peek at his emails before starting those few daily chores. That was a mistake!

The 5 minutes stretched into 30 because Joe got so involved in thinking about some of the messages. Joe didn't want to actually respond to any of the emails right away, but he did want to decide which ones to answer first and which to put off for the end of his workday.

My advice to Joe was to take care of his household chores first and not even look at his computer until they are done. Joe reluctantly agreed to try this for one week. When I next spoke to Joe, he told me that it was amazing! He was no longer wasting time preoccupied with thinking about how to respond to the emails he had seen. He got his chores done on time, and then he could give his full attention to his emails and answer them quickly and efficiently.

Julie Morgenstern, author of *Never Check Email in the Morning*, tells her readers to avoid the urge to multi-task. She says that even though you think you are getting more done when you are splitting your attention between multiple tasks, it is actually counterproductive. A study published in *The Journal of Experimental Psychology* indicates that it takes the brain four times longer to switch back and forth between projects than when it is focused on just one project. When you switch back and forth from one task to another it can take your brain several minutes to refocus on the original task—to remember where you left off and resume working with the same intensity as before. It's interesting to note that in 1740, Lord Chesterfield wrote a letter to his son giving him the following advice: "There is enough time for everything in the course of a day, if you do but one thing at once, but there is not enough time in the year, if you will do two things at a time." Christine Rosen quoted Lord Chesterfield in her article titled "The Myth of Multi-tasking" in the New Atlantis, number 20, Spring 2008. In a nutshell, you get more things done if you concentrate on doing one thing at a time!

Keep in mind that creating new habits is work. It doesn't happen overnight. It takes consistent practice to replace an old habit with a new one. Keep your goals in sight and remind yourself why you are changing your behaviors. In the book *Evolve the Brain*, Dr. Joe Dispenza explains that new habits are learned from mental practice and review. He says that "nerve cells that fire together wire together". New habits are made when nerve cells talk to each other often enough to make the brain form new connections. Dr. Dispenza goes on to explain that "nerve cells that don't fire together don't wire together". Old habits are broken by inhibiting the communication between those nerve cells often enough that the previous connections are broken. The more consistent you can be by practicing the new behavior the better chance you have of making it a habit.

Create Easy-to-Follow Daily Routines

How do you spend your time? Are you late getting to work? Do you find yourself racing to try and be on time to meet friends? Are there things you would like to get around to doing but never seem to find the time? You can solve these problems by creating new daily routines and developing new habits.

A routine is something you do every day without thinking. Routines are important to cultivate because they help you navigate portions of your day without thinking. I have a morning routine and an evening routine. In the morning, I get up, walk the dog, have breakfast with Nick, make the bed, shower, get dressed, water the plants, and complete my daily household chores before I begin my work day.

In the evening, I tidy my office, make my "To-Do" list for the next day, answer emails, and then I get ready for dinner with Nick. One of Nick's evening routines involves maintaining our computers. There is a series of things that he does regularly to ensure that our computers function as they should. Take a look at his suggestions for routine computer maintenance in Appendix F. You may want to add them to your own routine.

In addition to morning and evening routines, I have weekly routines I follow to tackle the laundry and other household chores. These morning, evening, and weekly routines do not make it onto my "To-Do" list because they are part of my day, every day. When you establish your own routines, certain chores may become part of your daily.ritual. For instance, when you come home, you should hang your coat in the closet. If you come home and just dump your coat over the back of a chair, you have created an extra step for yourself. When you are cleaning up the room you will have to hang up your coat. Why not just hang it up automatically and save yourself a step?

Another item to add to your routine is to make your bed every morning. It only takes a few minutes and it makes the bedroom look neat and tidy. When you change your clothes, put away the clothes you can wear again and put the dirty clothes directly into the laundry basket. This routine keeps the clean clothes from becoming rumpled and ensures the dirty laundry isn't left lying on the floor waiting for you to pick it up.

Think about your morning. Make a list of the things you would like to do everyday—routinely. The list should include a few things that will save you time in the long run. Tape the list to the bathroom mirror and leave it there until you no longer need to look at it.

Think about your evening, too. Make a list of the things you would like to incorporate into an evening routine. Tape the list to a kitchen cupboard or attach it to the refrigerator door. Leave it up until you don't need the reminder any more.

Sample Morning Routine
1. Get up
2. Exercise
3. Have breakfast
4. Do a few chores
5. Shower
6. Get dressed
7. Check emails
8. Go to work

Sample Evening Routine
1. Make a "To-Do" list for tomorrow
2. Take 15 minutes and put stray things away
3. Take 30 minutes to answer emails
4. Deal with today's paper mail
5. Tidy the kitchen counters
6. Charge cell phone
7. Pack bag for tomorrow
8. Put the "To-Do" list with my bag

Make a "To-Do" List Every Day

Have you ever had a sleepless night tossing and turning because your mind just won't stop? It just keeps working, thinking about all the things you meant to do today and simply can't forget to do tomorrow. Trying to keep track of all those tasks is preventing you from having a restful night's sleep. If this form of sleeplessness ever happens to you, I have a great solution! Every evening get out your paper and a pen or make a list on your computer. Think through your day. Was there something that you forgot to do or to pick up? Put that on your list.

Next think about the day to come. What are your appointments? Double check to make sure they are in your calendar.

Include errands on your list. Are there a few groceries to pick up? Do you need to go to the bank or to the cleaners. Is someone's birthday on your calendar? Maybe you need to get a gift, wrap it, and send it with a card in time to arrive on time.

If your list is on your computer, double check that it has synchronized with your phone. If you want, you can print it out so it will be at your fingertips in the morning. If it is already a paper list, put the list near the things you will be taking with you as you go about your day.

Prioritize the Items on Your List

Before I sit down to write my "To-Do" list, I think about the things I have to take care of. As these thoughts come to me and I write them down, I recognize that some things require more immediate attention than others. It is always best to take care of the most important and urgent things first. The other items can go to the bottom of the list and be done last or even put off to another day.

For instance, if a task must be completed by a certain time, I know it is urgent and I take care of it immediately. Sometimes items have specific dates attached, such as "RSVP by June 1st." Perhaps that date is a few weeks away, but responding to the invitation is a quick fix. If you can shoot off an email and finish the action by either tossing the invitation out or entering the information into your calendar, then do it as soon as possible. It will be one less thing you have to do later.

Generally, I have discovered that we all make time in our lives for the things we truly want to do even if there is no deadline or due date. You will determine for yourself how to construct your list. I admit that I put a few things on my list every day that I know have to be done, that take little time to complete, but that I don't really want to do.

Sometimes I arbitrarily assign these things a due date or deadline, because it encourages me to take care of them. I appreciate knowing they are over and done with. Putting things off for another time just delays the inevitable. Sooner or later you will find yourself doing the chore.

Another thing to consider when prioritizing is consequences. What happens if you don't do the task? Is there a negative consequence? Maybe there is an added incentive or benefit for completing the task promptly. My advice is to take these things into consideration when you make your list.

Here is one possible method to use when thinking about how to prioritize your "To-Do" list. Preface each phrase with "Things I…"
1. Want to do and must be done
2. Want to do and should be done
3. Don't want to do and must be done
4. Don't want to do and should be done

Use the chart below to help you rank the items on your "To-Do" list.

QUADRANT A	QUADRANT B
Want to do & must be done	Want to do & should be done
Don't want to do & must be done	Don't want to do & should be done

Now put the items from Quadrant A on your list first followed by those in Quadrant C. Chose the order in which to do the things in Quadrant B or Quadrant D and then add them to your list.

My client Debbie is a great example of how "To-Do" lists can simplify life. Debbie is a stay-at-home mom. She and her husband, Joe, have three children ages 10, 14, and 16. Their home in Atlanta is an older southern-colonial style. Debbie and Joe bought this house for its charm and decided they would undertake renovating it one area at a time. Debbie is in charge of overseeing these renovations. She also takes care of the family paperwork and bill paying. To complicate matters, Debbie recently moved her parents to Atlanta so that she could help take care of them. Debbie is a member of the "sandwich generation"– adults who are caring for their own children and for their parents.

Debbie called me because she was having trouble sleeping at night. She told me that she couldn't sleep because she had so much going on in her life that she had trouble relaxing. Debbie needed help getting on top of, in control of, her "To-Do" list.

At our first meeting I asked her to do a brain dump. This is simply writing down everything that is on your mind. Debbie's list was very long. Some of the things that were on her list were:
1. Parents' paperwork
2. Parents' bills
3. Parents' doctor appointments
4. After school activities for children
5. Grocery shopping and meal preparation
6. My bills
7. My paperwork
8. House renovation
9. Garden chores
10. Pets

As we went over Debbie's list, she discovered that some of the items on her list were occasional appointments—like taking her parents to the doctor. She had the flexibility to schedule those appointments at times when she was not busy with her children. Other items like bill paying and paperwork for her family and for her parents needed to be scheduled on a regular basis. Debbie decided that she could go to her parents' apartment a couple of times a week to pick up the bills and visit with her parents. These visits could happen around her children's school and activity schedule. She would plan to pay her parents' bills and do their filing one day a week. Debbie would also plan one day a week to follow up on her own bills and paperwork. For Debbie, these needed to be different days because she only wanted to allow an hour or two for these tasks.

I advised Debbie to take some time during the weekend to make a menu of meals for the coming week. The next step was to make a comprehensive grocery list, buying all the non-perishable items at once and scheduling other times during the week to pick up the few perishable items she would need to complete the meal.

My biggest piece of advice for Debbie was to take time every evening to review her day, and to make a comprehensive "To-Do" list for the next day. When I checked back with Debbie a few weeks later she told me that she was sleeping much better! She felt more in control of the activities in her life. Making her list every evening really helped her stay on track for the following day.

Plan Ahead

My son Alex was home recently for a visit. He told me that he really needed to schedule an evaluation with the allergist. Alex complained that the earliest appointment he could get was two months away, so he didn't book the time. I will be honest with you; I took him to task. I couldn't imagine that he would turn down the appointment.

Well, he wanted an appointment for the following week and was surprised that the allergist couldn't accommodate him. He was under the impression that making an appointment with a doctor was rather like making a reservation—a few days notice was all that was necessary.

Alex now understands that doctor appointments quite often need to be made well in advance. He is not used to planning ahead for things like this because I always used to make these appointments for him. Is planning ahead a new skill for you?

There are two different kinds of planning ahead: long-range and short-term. Long-range planning involves making plans for something that won't happen for a long time. For instance, you may find out in June about a professional conference scheduled to take place in December. Maybe attending the

Examples of Long-Range Planning Items

1. Doctor appointments
2. Business goals
3. Personal goals
4. Vacations

conference is a business goal for you. Here is what you need to do ahead of time:

1. Figure out how much it will cost. (Airfare, room, and conference fee)
2. Plan to save that amount of money. (Factor it into your budget.)
3. Schedule time off during those days.

Attending the conference is a reasonable goal, and conference attendees are often offered special "Early Bird" pricing when signing up in advance.

Examples of Short-term Planning Items

1. Chores for the week
2. Meal planning for the week
3. Errands
4. Appointments/ meetings
5. Special events

Short-term planning involves taking care of the things you know need to be done this week. I advise my clients to plan an hour on either Saturday or Sunday to think about the upcoming week. I tell them to list everything that absolutely has to be done during the next 5 or 6 days.

What are the appointments? Make sure they are in the calendar. What are the errands for the week? Some errands can be taken care of on your way to work, some during a lunch break, some on your way home. Figure out where you will be and then fit them into your schedule at convenient times. When planning, allow for travel time. Rushing to get somewhere on time is stressful. If you allow time for traffic or to catch public transportation, you arrive relaxed and ready for the meeting, appointment, or class. You may even arrive a few minutes early!

I like to be early, it gives me a chance to catch my breath and think about whatever is happening next.

Plan to do a do a few household chores each day. Taking care of your home a little bit at a time is easier and much less onerous than thinking about cleaning the whole place in one day. Why set aside an entire day to clean when designating an hour or less a few days each week will get the job done? A clean home is easier on the eye, and it is healthier too. Bacteria and allergens can't grow on clean surfaces. I have included sample cleaning routines for the bedroom, bathroom, living room, and kitchen in Appendix E. I also have listed some green (environmentally friendly) cleaning products you can buy and a few recipes I found for making your own green cleaning solutions.

The benefit to planning ahead is that it removes the guesswork of wondering how you are going to fit all the things you have to do into the week. This helps reduce stress. When you plan ahead to take care of a few things each day, you will not find yourself scrambling to get everything done at the last minute.

For instance, you may see your mother's birthday marked on your calendar. You can plan ahead by asking her for some gift ideas, buying the gift, wrapping it, and mailing it to her. That way you will not be stressed out the day before her birthday! Also, picture yourself at the grocery store. If you have taken the time to plan ahead and made a grocery list of the ingredients you need to prepare dinner, then you'll be less apt to forget anything important. It will also take you less time at the store because you won't be wandering the aisles searching for things you think you might need. If you have a list of errands with you, then you can plan ahead and do some errands on your way to the next place you need to be.

You will be efficient, saving time and gas, and avoiding stress.

Set Goals

Random House Dictionary defines the noun "goal" as "the result or achievement toward which effort is directed". Wandering aimlessly through the day is self-defeating. Questions like "What did I do today?" and "What is happening next?" will probably float through your mind. The benefit of setting goals is that a goal gives you purpose. It helps to define what you are working for.

When you begin to think about setting goals for yourself, be reasonable. Make sure they are achievable. Don't set your sights too high. If you do, you are setting yourself up for failure. Instead, set yourself up for success! It is so much more rewarding and encouraging to have successes—even if they are small ones. So, set a few short-term goals for yourself. For instance, checking your email only twice a day for one week, or getting to work 5 minutes early every day for a week, or waking up 15 minutes earlier every day so that you can have breakfast at home.

Put your goals in writing, decide on a date to reach each goal, and be accountable to yourself. If you have not accomplished your goal by the date set, cut yourself a little slack—forgive yourself—and make a new date. Once you have these goals conquered make new ones.

It is possible you will have to work a little harder to achieve them. Your next goal might be to finish a project, something that requires you to set aside time to devote to it. If it is a complicated project you will have to determine how much time you need— it's always better to overestimate than underestimate. Do something each week towards the completion of this project. You will be so happy with yourself when it is finished. For example, if your goal is to refinish a table you bought at a garage sale, you would probably not be able to do it all in one weekend. You should plan the steps you have to take. If the project requires three separate steps, plan to finish one each weekend.

At the end of 3 weeks you will have refinished the table and it will be better than ever!

A word of caution: work on only one goal at a time. If you are going to set multiple goals for yourself, understand that it is best to have each of the goals focused on a different aspect of your life: business, personal, or family. Having too many goals at once in a single sphere of life is distracting. Which one do you attack first?

If you find you have many goals that you really want to tackle, make yourself a list, figure out which aspect of your life the goals address, prioritize the goals, and then get to work.

Use an Extra Calendar

These days, many cell phones are like mini-computers. They hold our contact information and our calendar, and they can send reminders or sound alarms to indicate when appointments are about to begin. I advocate the use of one more calendar in addition to your phone.

My advice is to also use a large calendar where it is possible to view the details. It can be on your computer in a calendar program such as Microsoft Outlook or Google Calendar, or it may be a paper calendar. The computer programs are handy because, in most cases, your cell phone will link or sync with them. You can enter recurring events once and the computer will automatically remind you of the event every time it occurs.

For instance, if you have a weekly meeting every Monday at 8am, you enter the information once and it will appear in your computer calendar program every Monday at 8. The same is true for paying bills. If you enter the date you want to pay the bills, the computer will automatically fill in the information for each month going forward. As long as you remember to sync your computer with your phone, the information is stored in both places. You probably take your phone with you everywhere, so the information is always handy.

If you supplement your phone calendar with a paper calendar at your desk, you have to enter the information twice. Some people are just fine with that method. They like the action of writing things down, because it helps them to memorize the details. Use whichever method works for you, and keep your calendar with you to help you remember your appointments.

Schedule Personal Time

Throughout this chapter I have been talking about the use of time and the balance we all want to have in our lives. I have given advice about how to plan and set goals. Now, I want to give you permission to take time for yourself.

Some people feel guilty relaxing or taking time to have fun. I am one of those people. Having balance means taking time to work as well as time to play or to do something that enhances your quality of life.

Schedule time for yourself. Make an appointment with yourself, put it into your calendar, and then keep the appointment. Treat the appointments with yourself as you would any other appointment because they are just as important.

For example:
   _ go to the gym Monday and Thursday from 5:30–6:30pm
   _ sit and read a novel Tuesday evenings from 9:00–10:00pm
   _ take a long walk in the park Wednesdays at 5:00pm
   _ meet a friend for lunch on Saturday
   _ go to a museum on Sunday afternoon at 2:00pm

Be as specific as possible and set aside the time. These are the activities that make you happy and create a sense of balance in your life.

Set Boundaries

Most of us have phones that are multi-functional. We can receive calls, text messages, and emails wherever we are and all day and night long. The rule of working Monday through Friday from 9 to 5 no longer applies. Even if you work in an office there are probably many work related tasks that you can attend to at home on your own time. Where do you draw the line? Do you ever turn your phone off? Maybe it's a scary thought, that someone might not be able to reach you.

Creating boundaries shows respect for yourself, your family, and the people you contact. These limits help to distinguish between work and leisure. Boundaries let you schedule your activities efficiently so you can balance the different aspects of your life.

For example:
- Do not send a work-related message on a Saturday or Sunday.
- Make work-related calls between 9:00am and 6:00pm, Monday through Friday.
- Give at least 24 hours notice if you have to reschedule an appointment.
- Try not to work when you are on vacation.
- Set an auto-responder "away message" in your work related email.

There are always exceptions, but if you set boundaries and stick to them, you will find the balancing act less of a challenge.

"Etiquette is the science of living. It embraces everything. It is ethics. It is honor."

Emily Post

Chapter

Etiquette and You: Why it Matters

Etiquette... When you read this word, "etiquette," what picture pops into your mind's eye? Do you see a group of immaculately dressed women wearing white gloves and hats sitting at an elaborately set table drinking tea? Well, I understand you might think that etiquette is something old-fashioned, but it's really just the rules governing socially acceptable behavior for a given situation. You already use good etiquette when you cover your mouth before you sneeze or cough, when you stifle a burp, and when you say "excuse me." Do you ever ask what you're supposed to wear to a party? Sometimes the host and hostess would appreciate a tie and jacket or perhaps a cocktail dress. Other times, jeans and a t-shirt are appropriate. When you're out for dinner at a restaurant, or perhaps at a seated wedding reception, have you ever asked, "Is this my water?" or "Is this my butter plate?" Knowing where your water glass and butter plate are located at your place setting is part of etiquette or table manners.

When you write a formal email, I wonder if you ever ask yourself, quietly inside your head, what greeting to use. I believe that there are times for email messages to be informal and other times when the email can and should be as formal as a business letter that would be received via the postal service. Knowing when to send an informal message or a formal message is all part of email etiquette. There are some terrific books on manners and good social behavior, and I have listed them at the end of this chapter. My purpose here is to give you enough information so that as you embark on this newly independent life you have an understanding of how your behavior (etiquette) reflects on you.

Topics:

First Impressions
RSVP
Thank You Notes
Email Etiquette
Phone Etiquette

First Impressions

I know you aren't supposed to judge a book by its cover, but haven't you ever been drawn to open a book by the terrific graphics or artwork on a book jacket? I have. Similarly, if the cover is boring or unpleasant, you're likely to skip right over that book.

So what do you think when you have an appointment with someone you don't know and they show up looking unkempt? Are you wondering what I mean by that? Well, maybe this person's clothes are disheveled (part of his shirt is un-tucked, or his buttons are misaligned). You notice as you walk to meet this person that he shuffles his feet and looks at the floor. When you greet him, he mumbles a reply and barely shakes your hand. What impression do you come away with? Do you want to spend time with this person? From the way he greeted you it doesn't seem that this person is too interested in you, so why would you want to spend time with him?

Now, let's think about another person. This young man is nicely dressed and has a pleasant expression on his face. His clothes aren't fancy; they are just clean and nicely put together. He is walking towards you with a purposeful gait. In fact, he's looking directly at you. As he approaches, he puts his hand out, looks you in the eye and gives you a firm handshake. The two of you exchange a greeting. What's your impression this time? You can tell by the way this young man approached that he's interested in meeting with you. You can also tell that he gave some thought to his appearance.

Which one of these two men do you think you would want to spend an hour with during a meeting?

Whether you are going for a job interview or meeting someone for the first time, the way you approach them is critically important. You have just about 5 seconds to create interest, so use these seconds to your advantage. You have control over two important factors: your body language and the way you are dressed.

Dress appropriately for the situation. If it is a social situation and you're not sure what would be appropriate, check the invitation...the dress code is often listed there! If not, then ask your host or hostess. Going to work or on a job interview presents a different challenge. If you are a woman applying for a teaching position you should wear clothes that are neither too short nor too low-cut. If you are a man applying for a teaching position, business casual would be a good choice. Both men and women applying for a job at a bank, financial institution, or at a law office should wear formal business attire. But if you're applying for a job at an advertising agency, skip the business formal and try to be a little creative with your outfit! So, think about the position for which you are applying, think about the demands of the job, and then decide what form of dress is appropriate for the situation.

When you are at the interview, take control of your body language. Stand up straight and sit up straight in the chair—don't slump over or prop your elbow on the table in front of you. Keep a pleasant expression on your face (no matter what your inner voice is telling you) and look the interviewer in the eye.

One final note about first impressions: when you show interest in the person you are meeting, you create a lasting impression. It's OK to be friendly, but this doesn't mean you should ask personal questions. If this is a business meeting, know the history of the company and be prepared with a few questions of your own. You want to demonstrate that you've done your homework! If it is a social occasion keep in mind that you and the person you're meeting might have acquaintances in common. Maybe they know your mother?!

You never know where a connection will lead. If you make a good first impression, the person you're meeting might provide you with an introduction to a job lead, a club, or a volunteer organization to which you'd like to belong. But if you make a bad first impression, do you think that person is going to recommend you to others? Take the time, make the effort and make a good impression!

RSVP

Let's pretend you have just received an invitation to a party at someone's house. It doesn't matter if the invitation arrived in your email box or through the postal mail. What's important is what you do with that invitation.

The first thing you should do is think about whether or not you want to attend. My guess is that you know pretty much right away upon reading the invitation. Then, check your calendar. Are you free to attend on that day and time? Once you know whether or not you are interested and able to attend, it's important to let the host know promptly.

Are you wondering why it matters when you reply? Think about all the steps involved in planning a party. You pick a day and time to give your party. You determine where the party will be. It could be at your home, in a restaurant, at a club, a community center, or any other place you chose. You plan the menu. Then you invite your guests.
- Pick a day and time
- Choose a location (your home, a restaurant, a club, a community center, or some other location)
- Plan the menu
- Invite the guests

I'm simplifying the process; sometimes it's more involved and sometimes less. Here's the key point: once you've invited the guests to the party, you have to wait to see who responds so you know what the total number of guests will be. Until then, your hands are tied. You can't begin preparing food or buying party favors until you know how many people you are planning for.

Responding as soon as you know whether or not you will accept an invitation is showing good etiquette. When you don't respond until the very last possible second, it can look like you're waiting to see if you get a better invitation for that day. As in all situations, there are exceptions. Sometimes you just don't know what you're doing at that day and time because your plans may hinge on someone or something else.

As with invitations, it's also good etiquette to respond promptly to personal voice mail messages, text messages, and emails. This lets the individual writing or calling you know that you've received the message. Sometimes all the person wants is an acknowledgement.

I was talking with a friend the other day and she told me that getting in touch with her 20-something-year-old son is really difficult. He's told her not to leave voice mail messages on his phone because he never checks that message center (even though he says he can see on his phone that he's missed a call from his mother). So, she now sends him text messages. Unless she asks a direct question, her son doesn't reply, which she finds very frustrating.

I'm not suggesting that you must write lengthy messages in reply. What I am suggesting is that sometimes the sender doesn't even know if a message has been received. To remove all doubt, the recipient of the message can just write a short reply. It could even be just a smiley face if someone is sharing good news and you don't have time to elaborate. Think about how you feel when you're left wondering. Messages do sometimes get lost in cyber space!

Thank You Notes

When do you write Thank You notes? I write them (with a pen and paper) on a regular basis. I know I love receiving a kind note in the mail and so I figure other people like receiving them also. When my children were little, I coached them as they wrote Thank You notes to various aunts, uncles, grandparents, and friends upon receiving gifts for birthdays and Christmas. Now, I know they also write Thank You notes as a follow up to an interview. This is another way to create a good and lasting impression.

To be prompt, your follow up note to an interview should be in the form of an email message but it can also have a positive impact if it arrives in an envelope with a stamp. Are you asking yourself why that is? Well, consider this. It takes a far greater effort to pull out the stationery and actually put pen to paper, address the envelope, and put it in a mailbox. You may even do a few drafts of your note because, as we all know, there is no delete button when writing a note by hand.

Your note doesn't need to be long, just two or three paragraphs. The content will vary depending on whether it is a business note or a personal note.

Personal Thank You notes could be thanking someone for a nice weekend, a lovely dinner party or a thoughtful gift.

The first paragraph needs to reference what you're thanking the person for. Write a few sentences describing the gift, the weekend, or the dinner. Be sincere, be specific, and be sure that you are conveying true appreciation.

Your second paragraph can contain information about something you are doing. Share something personal with the recipient of your note—it could be business news, travel plans, or personal goals you feel like sharing.

Your final few sentences should reflect back on what you are thanking this person for and their thoughtfulness.

Business Thank You notes will be very different. A handwritten note is a nice extra touch, but it is important that you send a prompt email note as well. If your Thank You note to the interviewer is neither promptly received nor well-written, it is less likely that you will be considered for the job. A handwritten Thank You note may linger for many days in the mailroom while an email Thank You note will arrive quickly in the recipient's personal mailbox.

There are several occasions for which you should write a business Thank You note. They are: a job interview, an introduction or lead to a possible job connection, and guidance from a mentor or sponsor.

The construction of your note can be similar in nature to a personal Thank You note. In your opening paragraph, you want to thank the person for the time they spent with you. If this was during an interview, you should follow this up with a few sentences discussing why you now know you are a great fit for this job. Consider this note as your final pitch; a last chance to make yourself stand out as the best candidate for the position. Reaffirm your interest in the company and be sure to indicate your willingness to grow within the company. You can include a file attachment of your work—something not previously submitted with your application that you feel is relevant based on the discussion you had with the interviewer. You could also attach a relevant article from an outside source that you think would interest the interviewer and make you stand out. Finally, if you and the interviewer spoke about anything personal during your interview, like an upcoming vacation or event, be sure to reference that in your closing few sentences.

If you are writing to a colleague or peer to thank them for an introduction or a lead to a possible job, your note can be slightly less formal. You will still want to show sincere appreciation in your opening paragraph. You may also want to attach a relevant article—something you think your colleague is interested in. A possible end to your note could be an invitation to meet for coffee or a meal. Keep in mind that in order for the invitation to be sincere you should also suggest a time and place!

Email Etiquette

Let's talk about email etiquette. For example, what sort of greeting should you use in the emails you send? I recently received an email from someone seeking information about my organizing company. This person began their email with "Hey Diane, …" I replied to this person, but my first impression was not very positive. Consider your audience when constructing an email message.

There are a few other things to consider before you begin writing your message. They are:

Subject Line: Be specific in your subject line. Let the reader know as concisely as possible why you are writing this message. In fact, there are times when your subject line can contain the entire message—eliminating the need to even open the e-mail! An example of this is when you are answering a question. If the answer is a simple reply you can put that in your subject line. Follow the reply with either EOM (End Of Message) or NT (No Text) to be really clear.

Language: Is this a formal or informal letter? Does your sentence structure need to be correct or can you communicate in abbreviated phrases or slang? Should you check your spelling? If this is a formal business letter you will want to let the person receiving your message know that communications from you will be easy to understand, complete, and grammatically correct.

Greeting: Think about how you would address the recipient in a hand-written note. Would you begin your note with "Dear"? You should address your email message in a similar fashion depending on how well you know the person. In some cases, "Dear..." is appropriate. For less formal messages "Hello" or "Hi" may work. It will depend on your relationship with the recipient of your message.

Closing: Generally speaking you can end your message with a closing similar to the one in the message to which you are replying. For example, if the message you received closed with "Regards" followed by their professional signature you can do the same thing. If it is a business message and you are initiating the communication you could sign off with "Sincerely" followed by your full name and then your professional signature.

One final thing to remember is that your email message represents you. It's really difficult to interpret or understand a message if the language isn't clear. After all, you don't hear the tone of voice as you would in a phone conversation.

Cell Phone Etiquette

Do you use a smart phone? I think that many of us probably can't imagine how we managed our lives without our cell phone. We can now connect to the Internet whenever we want to, wherever we happen to be. With a smart phone, we can reply to email, send text messages, or call anyone we need to reach. With the right applications in our phones we can get directions based on our current location. Is there ever a time when we are without our phones?

Well, with that thought in mind, let's look at when it is and isn't appropriate to use our phones. In other words, what is good phone etiquette? There are definitely times when your cell phone should be either turned off or simply ignored. Are you shouting "NO!" at me? I understand. We have become so connected to these devices that the mere thought of not using them at will might be a little scary but please hear me out. You may even come to agree with me.

Places you should not use your cell phone:
- Dinner
- Meetings and Performances (movies, plays, etc.)
- Bathroom
- Driving

Dinner:
Have you ever been out for dinner and seen two people sitting across from one another at a table looking, not at each other, but at their cell phones? They might be checking mail messages and replying or texting other people. Maybe they are on a social media site, who knows? The point is they are not talking to each other. They could be eating alone. When you are dining with someone, either in a restaurant or a home, put your phone away; essentially disconnect yourself for that time. Sharing a meal and conversation is wonderful and fun. Be present with that person or those people and enjoy the meal. The exception to this, and there are exceptions to everything, is an emergency. For example, if the babysitter calls, you need to respond!

Meetings and Performances:
When you go to a meeting do you keep your phone on silent so that if you get a call, a text message, or an email your phone vibrates? If you do this, do you then quietly take your phone out and reply? I was presenting a workshop a few months ago and this happened to me. Several times during my talk someone would take their phone out, read the screen, and then start typing to reply. I admit I wondered if my workshop was not holding their attention. I decided not to take it personally but it made me wonder how the attendees could learn the material being presented and respond on their phones at the same time.

If you are attending a meeting, a lecture, a movie, a play—
wherever you are participating as the member of an audience—
put your phone away. Disconnect yourself for that length of time.
Give the show or the speaker your full and undivided attention.
You will get more out of it, I promise! As in the dinner example,
there is always an exception. If there is a real emergency, quietly
leave the room and respond. This way you are responding
to the message but still being respectful to the speaker, the
performance, and the other members of the audience.

Bathroom:
Let's say you are in a public restroom and your phone rings. Do
the right thing and let it go to your voicemail. The person calling
you will be happy you waited. Return the call when you have
left the restroom. The other people in the restroom do not want
to be the unwilling eavesdroppers on your conversation. You
probably do not take your phone with you when you are using
the bathroom at home, so do everyone a favor and ignore your
phone if it rings when you are in a public bathroom.

Driving:
Research shows that talking on the phone takes your attention
away from other tasks. Remember that when you decide to talk
on the phone while driving your car. Even if your cell phone is
linked to a system in your car allowing your phone to be hands
free, keep your conversations short and non-controversial. If you
think you're about to have a lengthy and involved conversation,
find a place to pull over and park. This way you will be able
to concentrate on the conversation and won't have to think
about the other cars on the road. Certainly, it's handy to be able
to make calls from your car. If I'm stuck in heavy traffic, I'll
give my client a call to let them know I'm on my way. It's also

wonderful to have in case of an accident or other emergency. My advice to you is to keep your cell phone activity in the car limited to essential calls. While we're talking about cell phones and cars please do not ever text while driving. In some states it's illegal to talk on the phone or text while driving. If caught doing so by the police, such actions can result in a very hefty fine, not to mention the price paid by all involved if an accident were to occur as a result. Enough said.

I was discussing this part of my book with my family, and I got an interesting comment from my sister-in-law Joan. She told me that she almost hit a pedestrian who was talking on his cell phone while walking through a parking lot. The story goes like this: Joan was slowly and carefully backing out of a parking space, looking behind her and to either side. Nothing was coming. Joan said she did see a man walking in the parking lot, talking on his cell phone, but he was nowhere near her car. Thankfully, Joan continued to check around her car as she backed up, because the man suddenly appeared right behind her! He was winding his way between cars and concentrating so hard on his conversation that he had clearly not noticed that her car was moving. Since Joan was paying attention, she was able to stop quickly and avoid bumping him. Her suggestion is to only have brief conversations if you are walking and talking on the phone. Both drivers and pedestrians should pay attention to their surroundings.

Table Manners

What constitutes good etiquette or good social behavior at a dinner table? There are a few obvious behaviors to mention. Someone probably told you about them from the time you first started eating food.

Chewing:
Take small enough bites of food so that your mouth is not over-
stuffed. Chew your food thoroughly so that you don't choke.
Also, very importantly, chew with your mouth closed. No one
wants to see the contents.

Talking:
It always happens that someone will ask me a question just
as I've taken a bite of my food. Has that ever happened to
you? What should you do? I can only tell you what I do. The
temptation is to just go ahead and answer the question—sort
of pushing the contents in my mouth to one side. I resist that
temptation and instead hold up my hand to indicate I'll answer as
soon as I can. Usually, the person asking the question does so not
knowing I have just put food in my mouth and they appreciate
my delay in responding.

Posture:
Try to sit up straight at the table. Sit with your back against the
back of the chair and your hands naturally in your lap. Elbows
don't belong on the table nor do your forearms. Sitting up
straight keeps you alert and can aid in your digestion.

Table setting:
Have you ever been to a formal dinner and had the person sitting
next to you say, "Is this my water?" or "Is this my butter plate?"
Very simply, your water is always the glass on the right side of
your place setting. It is above your knife. Your butter plate is
above your fork on the left hand side of your place setting or
above your left hand. I have included a labeled formal place
setting for you to refer to.

Wherever you go for a meal, whether it is at someone's house, a fast food restaurant, a fancy restaurant, or a formal event, good table manners are noticed and appreciated. One of the first things to do when you sit down is to put your napkin in your lap. This signals the beginning of the meal. If you have a host or hostess at your table, you only begin eating when they pick up their utensil. This happens at the beginning of each course of the meal. Your host or hostess will wait to begin eating until everyone has been served. The meal is over when the host or hostess puts their napkin on the table.

Having good etiquette will serve you well in all situations. No one will ever comment that it's too bad that you have such good manners. But they will notice immediately if you have bad manners or if you create a bad impression. When you create a bad impression, you have to work hard to erase it and replace it with a good impression. When you create a good impression, it's easy to build on that to forge solid relationships.

Etiquette Book List

The Etiquette Book: A Complete Guide to Modern Manners
Jodi R. R. Smith

Emily Post's Etiquette, 18th Edition
Peggy Post (Author)
Anna Post (Author)
Lizzie Post (Author)
Daniel Post Senning (Author)

The Little Book of Etiquette (Hardcover)
Dorothea Johnson (Author)

Multicultural Manners: Essential Rules of Etiquette for the 21st Century (Paperback)
Norine Dresser (Author)

Letitia Baldrige's New Manners for New Times: A Complete Guide to Etiquette (Hardcove)
Letitia Baldrige (Author)
Denise Cavalieri Fike (Illustrator)

The Amy Vanderbilt Complete Book of Etiquette: 50th Anniversary Edition (Hardcover)
Nancy Tuckerman (Author)
Nancy Dunnan (Author)

Resources

Books:

- *Evolve the Brain* by Dr. Joe Dispenza
- *Organize Your Office in No Time* by Monica Ricci
- *Organizing From the Inside Out* by Julie Morgenstern
- *Never Check E-mail in the Morning* by Julie Morgenstern
- *Simplify Your Time: Stop Running & Start Living* by Marcia Ramsland
- *The Well-Ordered Home* by Kathleen Kendall-Tackett, Ph.D

Websites:

The following websites are listed in the order in which they appear in the book:

Organizing Your Move:
- interiordec.about.com – For ideas about decorating the interior of your home
- 1stdibs.com – More ideas for decorating
- usps.gov – United States Postal Service (for forwarding or holding your mail)
- oneswitch.com – To simplify sending your new address to all your magazine subscription.
- realsimple.com/er – Create an Emergency Card for your wallet

Organizing Your Kitchen:
- epicurious.com – Great recipes
- foodnetwork.com – Great recipes
- realsimple.com/recipes – Great recipes
- fightbac.org – The Partnership for Food Safety
- fsis.usda.gov – The USDA Food Safety and Inspection Service

Organizing Your Budget:
- money-rates.com/savings.htm – Compare savings account rates at different financial institutions
- money.howstuffworks.com/personal-finance/401k.htm – Explains how 401k plans work
- cdrates.bankaholic.com – Compares CD rates at different financial institutions
- money.cnn.com/pf/ – Articles detailing how and where to invest your money for steady growth
- fool.com/investing/basics – Investing advice and information

Organizing Your Papers:
www.containerstore.com – Organizing accessories www.kangaroomstorage.com – Organizing accessories www.seejanework.com – Organizing accessories www.levenger.com – Organizing accessories
www.officecandy.com – Organizing accessories

Note: *please check my website (www.dnqsolutions.com) and click on the Now What? Link for updated website information.*

Appendix A

Linen Shopping List
- Pillows – 2
- Pillow protectors
- Mattress pad
- Sheets – 2 sets (each set has a fitted sheet, a top sheet, and 2 pillow cases)
- Blanket
- Quilt or duvet
- Duvet cover
- Bath towels – 2 sets (each set has a bath towel, a hand towel, and a wash cloth)
- Dish towels – 2 or 3 to dry dishes
- Oven mitts – 2

Appendix B

Essential Household Items
- Toilet paper
- Hand soap
- Bucket
- Toilet brush
- Sponge
- Plunger
- Mop
- Broom
- Dustpan & small handheld brush
- Kitchen garbage can with a lid
- Garbage bags
- Recycling receptacle – This can be another garbage can that is designated as recycling
- 2 wastebaskets – 1 for the bathroom, 1 for the bedroom
- Vacuum
- Flashlights
- Batteries
- Battery operated radio
- Batteries for the radio
- Candles
- Matches
- Small collapsible step stool
- Paper towels
- Plastic wrap
- Aluminum foil
- Wax paper

- Sandwich bags
- Food storage bags
- Smoke and carbon monoxide detectors
- Batteries for the detectors (change these batteries once a year)
- Fire extinguisher – Keep it in your kitchen

Appendix C
Recipes from Joan's Kitchen

Lunch/Brunch Suggestions:

• Granola
• Frittata (similar to an omelet)
• Soup – Chicken Noodle Soup, Minestrone Soup
• Salad – can be a side dish or the main meal

Granola

3 cups old-fashioned rolled oats
2 cups raw or roasted nuts* (use your favorite)
1 cup organic coconut chips
1 cup dried fruit (use your favorite)
2/3 cup pure maple syrup
1/3 cup extra virgin olive oil
1/3 cup light brown sugar
1 tsp. kosher salt
½ tsp. ground cinnamon

Preheat oven to 300 degrees. In a large bowl combine oats, nuts (only if raw), coconut chips, maple syrup, olive oil, brown sugar, salt, and cinnamon. Spread mixture on a rimmed baking sheet lined with parchment paper. Bake for 20 minutes, remove from oven, and add dried fruit (and any nuts that are not raw). Stir well. Bake for an additional 20-25 minutes (until golden brown). Cool, place in airtight container.

If the nuts are raw, I add them at the onset of baking. If they are already roasted, I add them with the dried fruit during the last 20 minutes of baking.

There are endless combinations of nuts and dried fruit to experiment with. One of our favorite combinations is pumpkin seeds, pistachios, and dried cherries.

Frittata

8 large eggs
3 tbsp. heavy cream
½ tsp. salt
¼ tsp. freshly ground black pepper
1-½ tbsp. butter
½ cup diced yellow onions
½ cup sliced white mushrooms
½ cup diced green bell peppers
½ cup diced red bell peppers
½ cup diced ham
2 tbsp. chopped green onions (tops only), more to garnish
1-½ tsp. minced garlic
2 tbsp. chopped fresh parsley leaves

¾ cup shredded cheese (try a combination of cheddar and Monterey jack cheese, or if you like a little kick, try substituting pepper jack cheese)

Preheat the broiler and place the top rack 4 to 5 inches from the heating element.

In a large bowl, whisk together the eggs, cream, ¼ tsp. of salt, and 1/8 tsp. of the pepper until the eggs are frothy. Set aside. In a 10-inch nonstick ovenproof skillet, melt the butter over medium high heat.

Add the onions, mushrooms, green and red bell peppers and cook, stirring, until they are soft, 3 to 4 minutes. Add the ham and stir well.

Add the green onions, garlic, parsley, remaining salt and pepper and cook, stirring, until the garlic is fragrant, about 30 seconds. With the pan over medium heat, pour the egg mixture over the vegetables and ham.

Sprinkle the shredded cheese evenly on top.

Cook, lifting with a rubber spatula to let the eggs flow underneath, until the edges are set but the middle is loose, 3 to 4 minutes.

Remove skillet from the heat and place under the broiler until the eggs are slightly puffed and the cheese is golden brown, 2 to 3 minutes. Do not overcook.

Remove skillet from the oven and carefully slide the frittata out onto a large serving platter.

Garnish with additional chopped parsley and green onions, if desired. Serve with a nice green salad.

Serves 6

Chicken Noodle Soup
(the ultimate comfort food)

One 3-½ to 4-½ lb. chicken
Cold water
2 medium onions, peeled and quartered
1 cup carrots peeled and sliced
½ cup celery, leaves included, sliced
1 parsnip, peeled and sliced
10 peppercorns
1 bay leaf, crumbled
1 cup parsley, chopped coarsely (reserve 2 tbsp.)
1 tsp. salt
¼ tsp. ground pepper
8 oz. egg noodles

Place the chicken in a stockpot and cover with cold water.

Bring to a boil and skim foam.

Add ½ cup carrots, the celery, parsnip, onions, peppercorns, bay leaf, parsley, salt, and pepper.

Reduce the heat and simmer, partially covered, until chicken is cooked, about 2 hours.

Remove the chicken to a plate. When cool enough to handle, remove skin and bones and discard them.

Shred meat and set aside.

Strain soup through a fine sieve or cheesecloth-lined colander into a clean pot and discard vegetables.

Add remaining carrots to broth and simmer 5 minutes.

Add egg noodles* and simmer an additional 7 minutes, until carrots are tender and noodles are cooked.

Add chicken and reserved parsley. Season to taste with salt and pepper.

Serves 6

*If you plan on freezing your leftover soup or don't think you'll be consuming your leftover soup within a day or two, don't add the egg noodles at this time, but instead cook them separately until al dente and add directly to individual bowls of soup. One reason for this is that the noodles tend to soften and become mushy when frozen and reheated. Another reason is that the noodles, when added to the soup pot uncooked, absorb a good deal of the chicken stock while cooking. I always cook the noodles separately and add just before serving.

Freeze the soup (without noodles) and when you're ready to have it again, defrost, reheat, and add leftover cooked rice or al dente pasta.

Minestrone Soup

4 oz. ditalini pasta (or try orecchiette, a small ear-shaped pasta) Extra-virgin olive oil
6 cups homemade or low-sodium chicken stock
¼ lb. diced pancetta* (Italian specialty meat made from pork)
3 cloves of garlic, minced
1 cup diced carrots
1 cup diced celery
2 small yellow onions, chopped
1 tbsp. fresh rosemary, chopped
1 can (14-½ oz.) diced tomatoes
1 can (15-½ oz.) cannellini beans (white kidney) drained and rinsed
1 large potato, peeled and diced
4 medium zucchini, diced
Salt and freshly ground pepper
Freshly grated parmesan cheese (for garnish)

*Pancetta can usually be found with other packaged Italian meats such as salami and prosciutto. Check with the butcher or deli department in your local market if you can't find it.

Heat ¼ cup olive oil in a large saucepan over medium-high heat. Add the pancetta and cook until it begins to brown, 3 to 4 minutes. Add the garlic and cook about 30 seconds, stirring constantly.

Lower the heat to medium and add the carrots, celery, and onions. Cook until the vegetables are soft, 8 to 10 minutes, stirring often.

Add the chopped rosemary.

Add the tomatoes, beans, diced potato, and zucchini.

Raise the heat to high.

Add the chicken stock and bring to a boil.

Lower the heat to a simmer and cook until the diced potatoes are tender, about 10 minutes.

While the soup is simmering, bring a large pot of salted water to a boil over high heat.
Add the pasta and cook according to package directions. Drain.

A few minutes before serving, add the pasta to the soup.

Season to taste with freshly ground pepper and salt.

Serve with a drizzle of extra virgin olive oil and a sprinkle of freshly grated Parmesan cheese. Enjoy with a nice crusty loaf of bread.

Serves 6–8

There's no need to purchase bottled salad dressing when it's so easy to make at home. A good bottle of extra virgin olive oil and some red wine or balsamic vinegar are all you need. We usually dress our salad with a drizzle of extra virgin olive oil, a splash or two of red wine vinegar, a little minced garlic, salt, and freshly ground pepper to taste. It's simple and delicious without the added preservatives.

Basic Vinaigrette Dressing

1 garlic clove, minced
¼ tsp. salt
1 tbsp. Dijon mustard
¼ cup red wine or balsamic vinegar
¾ cup extra virgin olive oil Freshly ground black pepper

Mince garlic and mash with salt.
In a small bowl, whisk garlic paste, mustard, and vinegar.

Slowly add the extra virgin olive oil, whisking constantly, until the dressing is emulsified.

Toss with greens and season with freshly ground black pepper to taste.

Refrigerate any leftover dressing and use within a few days (be sure to bring to room temperature before using).

There are also salad dressings made with fresh squeezed citrus juice (lemon or orange) and even a summer salad dressing made with fresh raspberries.

A package of mixed baby greens or baby spinach with a balsamic dressing and some chopped apple or pear—or even dried cranberries or cherries, and a few roasted nuts (pine, walnut, or sliced almonds)—sprinkled on top is wonderful. Add a little crumbled blue cheese and you've got a very satisfying side dish. Add some sliced grilled chicken or beef, maybe even a hard-boiled egg, and you have a meal.

Our "house salad" consists of romaine lettuce, baby arugula, chopped tomato, chopped cucumber, chopped red pepper, and red onion. Sometimes we'll add chopped avocado.

Dinner Suggestions:

Stir-Fry Dinner
Pasta dish – Farfalle with tomato and sausage
Chicken dish
   - Basic roast chicken
   - Chicken parmesan sandwich
Meat dish – Cheesy hamburgers
Fried Rice – a good way to use leftover vegetables & meat

Stir-fry Dinner

Sesame Oil
Minced garlic
Fresh mixed vegetables (or a bag of frozen) such as broccoli
    florets, red pepper & asparagus (cut into 1 inch pieces)
Chicken broth
Hoisin sauce
Oyster sauce
Boneless chicken breast or pork tenderloin thinly sliced

Start with a little sesame oil in your wok or frying pan over medium-high heat.

Add a teaspoon of minced garlic and stir for about 30 seconds.

Add fresh mixed vegetables (or a bag of frozen) such as broccoli florets, red pepper, and asparagus (cut in 1-inch pieces).

Add a few tablespoons of chicken broth. Cover and simmer for about 2–3 minutes.

Remove vegetables to a bowl and cover to keep warm.

Add a tablespoon of sesame oil to the pan. When the oil is hot, add the chicken or pork along with some chopped green onion or sliced yellow onion.

Stir-fry for 3–4 minutes until your meat is no longer pink.

Return the mixed vegetables to the pan.

Add 3–4 tablespoons of hoisin sauce, 1 tablespoon of oyster sauce, and 2–3 tablespoons of chicken broth.

Toss until evenly coated with sauce.

Season to taste with salt and pepper.

Serve with steamed rice.

Garnish this with chopped green onions, roasted peanuts or roasted cashews, if desired.

Farfalle with Tomato and Sausage

2 tbsp. olive oil
½ medium onion, chopped
3 cloves garlic, chopped
1 can (28 oz.) whole tomatoes
½ cup heavy cream (add a little more for a richer sauce)
1 lb. Italian sausage, casings removed, crumbled and cooked
½ tsp. crushed red pepper flakes
3 tbsp. finely chopped parsley
1 box (16 oz) Farfalle or bow tie pasta
Freshly grated Parmesan cheese

Heat olive oil in a large skillet.

Add onion and garlic and cook until softened, about 5 minutes.

Add tomatoes (crushed with your hands or broken up with the back of a spoon), cream, sausage, and red pepper flakes. Simmer for 10 minutes.

Cook bow tie pasta according to package directions. Drain pasta and toss with sauce.

Sprinkle with chopped parsley and Parmesan cheese before serving. Serve with a salad and crusty loaf of bread.

Serves 4–6

Basic Roast Chicken

One 6 ½ to 7 lb. roasting chicken
½ cup (1 stick) butter, room temperature
2 tbsp. chopped fresh rosemary
3 large garlic cloves, minced
1 ½ tsp. lemon zest
¼ cup dry white wine
1 cup low sodium chicken broth
2 tbsp. all purpose flour
Lemon wedges
Rosemary or thyme sprigs

Combine butter, rosemary, garlic, and lemon zest in a small bowl. Season with salt and pepper. Reserve 2 tablespoons of the mixture.

Preheat oven to 450°F.

Rinse chicken; pat dry.
Carefully slide hand under skin of chicken breast to loosen skin from meat. Rub half of herb butter over chicken breasts under skin.

Spread remaining herb butter over outside of chicken.

Season chicken with salt and pepper.

Place a lemon wedge, a sprig of rosemary or thyme and a clove or two of garlic into the cavity and tie legs.

Place chicken in a heavy large roasting pan.

Roast 20 minutes.

Reduce oven temperature to 375°F.

Roast chicken until meat thermometer inserted into thickest part of inner thigh registers 175°F, about 1 hour 30 minutes. You can also pierce the thickest section of the legs with a fork. If the juices run clear, the chicken is cooked.

Lift chicken and tilt to empty juices into roasting pan.

Transfer chicken to platter and tent with aluminum foil to keep warm.

Pour pan juices into a large glass measuring cup and wait for fat to separate, about 10 minutes. Spoon fat off top.

Add wine to pan and place over high heat.
Bring wine to boil, scraping up any browned bits.

Pour wine mixture into cup with pan juices.

Melt reserved 2 tablespoons herb butter in saucepan over medium-high heat. Add flour and whisk until smooth, about 3 minutes.

Gradually whisk in pan juices and ½ cup of chicken broth

Boil until thickened, 5 to 8 minutes.

If gravy becomes too thick, add a little more chicken broth to thin.

Season gravy with salt and pepper.

Arrange sliced lemon and rosemary or thyme sprigs around chicken on platter. Serve with gravy.

Serves 6

VARIATION: Add a couple of peeled and quartered potatoes during the last 45 minutes of cooking time. Toss with pan juices and cook until golden brown.

Chicken Parmesan Sandwich

2 medium tomatoes
4 kaiser or other hard rolls
¼ cup breadcrumbs
¼ cup grated parmesan cheese
¾ tsp. oregano
¼ tsp. pepper
4 chicken cutlets, thin sliced
2 tbsp. olive oil Mayonnaise
Several leaves of lettuce
1 avocado

Slice the tomatoes and the avocado.

Cut the rolls in half.

In a plastic bag, combine the breadcrumbs, parmesan cheese, oregano, and pepper.

Add the chicken cutlets and toss to coat them lightly.

In a large skillet, warm the olive oil over medium heat until hot but not smoking.

Add the chicken and sauté until browned and cooked through, about 4 minutes per side. Add more oil, if necessary, to prevent sticking.

Remove the chicken to a plate. Tent with foil to keep warm.

Spread the 2 halves of each roll with mayonnaise.

Put the chicken on one half of the roll.

Arrange the lettuce, tomato, and avocado beside the roll on each plate.

Serves 4

Cheesy Hamburgers

2 cups grated Monterey Jack or Pepper Jack cheese
1 medium onion
1 pound ground round
2 tbsp. Worcestershire sauce or steak sauce
1 tsp. coarsely ground pepper
½ teaspoon salt

Finely chop the onion

Combine in a medium bowl the beef, onion, Worcestershire sauce, ¼ tsp. of pepper, and the salt and mix gently.

Divide the hamburger mixture into 4 equal portions.

Flatten each portion of hamburger into a patty and press one-fourth of the cheese into the center.

Pull the sides of the hamburger patty up and over the cheese to completely enclose it. Gently reform into a flat patty, making sure the cheese does not poke out.

Sprinkle the hamburger patties with the remaining pepper.

In a large non-stick frying pan, cook the hamburgers over medium-high heat until done, about 4 minutes per side for medium and 5 minutes per side for well-done.

Serves 4

Serving suggestion: either serve on rolls (sliced in half) with sliced tomatoes and lettuce or serve with a mixed green salad and a small baked potato.

Fried Rice

This is a great recipe if you have leftovers that you want to eat in a different way. It is also good if you just feel like having fried rice. Start with cold cooked rice; if it is warm or hot the grains will stick together.

2 cups cold cooked rice
2 eggs
¼ cup salad oil
1 small onion, chopped
1 clove garlic, minced
1 medium green pepper, seeded and diced
1-½ cups cooked ham, chicken, turkey, or pork
½ cup roasted salted peanuts (optional)
2 tbsp. soy sauce
Lemon wedges, tomato wedges, and cucumber slices

In a small bowl, lightly beat together the eggs.

Place a wok (or large frying pan) over medium heat; when the wok is hot, add 1 tablespoon of the oil.
When the oil is hot, add the eggs.

Stir the eggs until softly scrambled; remove them from the wok and set aside.

Add 1 tablespoon of oil to the wok.

When the oil is hot, add the onion and garlic. Stir-fry until the onions are soft.

Add the green pepper (and/or any leftover vegetables you have in the refrigerator) and 1-½ cups of meat and peanuts.

Stir-fry until heated through (about 2 minutes) remove from wok and set aside.

Pour remaining 2 tablespoons of oil into the wok.

When the oil is hot, add the rice and stir-fry until heated through. Stir in vegetable and meat mixture and soy sauce. Add eggs and stir gently until the eggs are mixed in.

Garnish the plates with lemon, tomato, and cucumber.

Serves 4

Dessert?

Here is a very simple no-fail cake recipe. I call it Wacky Cake because it is made with oil and vinegar. It is a really moist cake that you can serve on its own or with a little vanilla ice cream on the side.

Wacky Chocolate Cake

1-½ cups all-purpose flour
1 cup sugar
¼ cup unsweetened cocoa
1 tsp. baking soda
½ tsp. salt
1 cup water
¼ cup plus 2 tbsp. vegetable oil
1 tbsp. vinegar
1 tsp. vanilla

Preheat oven to 350°.

Grease and flour a 9-inch layer pan or an 8-inch square pan.

Combine flour, sugar, cocoa, baking soda and salt in a large mixing bowl.

Add water, oil, vinegar, and vanilla.

Mix together with a spoon or whisk until the batter is smooth and well blended. Pour into the prepared pan.

Bake for 35–40 minutes or until a toothpick inserted in the center comes out clean.

Serves 6–9

Appendix D
Green Cleaning Products and Recipes

___

If you decide to clean your home in an eco-friendly way, there are many options. Environmentally friendly cleaning products are readily available in most supermarkets. You can also make your own. The ingredients are generally available at supermarkets or drugstores. Whether you make your own products or buy commercially made products, you need to follow some basic safety guidelines.

Safety Guidelines:

1. Store all cleaners out of reach of children and pets.
2. Keep cleaning products away from heat—many are flammable.
3. Never mix cleaners that contain bleach with those that contain ammonia. Mixing them together can form a deadly, toxic gas.

Make Your Own Green Cleaning Solutions

Ingredients:
- Borax
- White vinegar
- Rubbing alcohol
- Baking soda
- Hydrogen peroxide (3% solution)
- Spray bottles to hold the solutions you make

The following ideas and preparations are excerpted from the Quamut Guide on Cleaning Your Home.

Mild All-purpose Cleaner:
Mix equal parts water and white vinegar in a spray bottle.

Glass Cleaner:
Mix equal parts rubbing alcohol, water, and white vinegar.

Mildew Cleaner:
Mix equal parts water and hydrogen peroxide.

Scouring Cleanser:
Use baking soda—it is abrasive and does a really good job!

Appendix E
Sample Weekly Cleaning Routine

Clean the Bathroom
Time allotted: about 30 minutes

Bring the cleaning supplies you need and put them in the hall just outside the bathroom:
- Vacuum
- Paper towels
- All-purpose bathroom cleaner
- Glass cleaner—look for one that has vinegar in it, or make your own (see previous appendix)
- Toilet bowl cleaner
- Bucket
- Sponge

Procedure to Follow:
Fill the bucket about 1/3 full with warm water. Add some all-purpose antibacterial liquid cleaner. You will use this mixture to wash with.

Step 1: Remove used towels. If you have a washer and dryer either in your home or in your building, take the towels and put them in the washer. Begin the wash cycle for towels. By the time you have finished cleaning the bathroom, it will be time to put the towels in the dryer!

Step 2: Apply the toilet bowl cleaner around the inside of the toilet bowl and just let it sit for now.

Step 3: Remove everything from the counter top around the sink and above the toilet.

Step 4: Spray the mirrors with glass cleaner and use a paper towel to clean the mirrors.

Step 5: Wash the inside of the sink and the counter top with the mixture in the bucket.

Step 6: Dry the counter top, the inside of the sink, and the faucets—this will keep them shiny!

Step 7: Put back only the items that you really want to keep out—put the rest away under the sink.

Step 8: Wash the inside of the bathtub, including the walls enclosing the shower, with the mixture in the bucket. You may need to also use a cleaning agent to remove soap scum.

Step 9: Wash the top of the toilet tank, the toilet seat (on top and underneath), and the outside of the toilet bowl with the mixture in the bucket. Use a toilet brush to clean the inside of the toilet.

Step 10: Vacuum the bathroom rug and put it in the hall outside the bathroom.

Step 11: Vacuum the bathroom floor and then mop the floor.

Step 12: Put fresh towels on the towel bars and put the bathroom rug back in place. Remember to put the towels in the dryer and then take a well-deserved break while they dry!

Step 13: Remove the towels from the dryer, fold them and put them away.

Step 14: Put cleaning supplies away

Clean the Bedroom
Time allotted: 15-20 minutes

Bring the cleaning supplies you need to your bedroom.
- Vacuum
- Dusting cloth—old athletic socks are great dusting cloths!
- Furniture cleaner
- Glass cleaner & paper towels (for any non-wood furniture)

Steps to Follow:

Step 1: Remove the sheets from your bed and start them in the wash if possible.

Step 2: Put fresh sheets on your bed and make your bed.

Step 3: Remove everything from the top of your bureau.

Step 4: Spray a little furniture cleaner on your dusting cloth and then dust the top, front, and sides of your bureau.

Step 5: Put back on top of your bureau only those things that you want to keep there. Put the other things back where they belong.

Step 6: Repeat steps 3, 4, and 5 for all the other furniture in your room.

Step 7: Vacuum your bedroom and the hall outside. As you vacuum, remember to vacuum things like windowsills and baseboards using the soft brush attachment.

Step 8: Put your sheets in the dryer. Take a break while your sheets dry!

Step 9: Put your cleaning supplies away.

Step 10: Remember to remove your sheets from the dryer when they are done, fold them, and put them away.

Clean the Living Room & Dining Area
Time allotted: 15-20 minutes

Bring the cleaning supplies you need to the living room.
- Vacuum
- Cleaning cloth
- Furniture polish
- Glass cleaner & paper towels

Steps to Follow:

Step 1: Clean front and back of TV and any other electronics with a paper towel & glass cleaner. Spray a tiny bit of glass cleaner on the paper towel and carefully dust the electronics. A little bit of spray goes a long way! You don't want to spray the electronics directly—the idea is to pick up the dust with the paper towel.

Step 2: Dust the TV stand. You do not need to remove all the electronics from the stand to dust each shelf. If you can gently lift the electronics and reach under them to dust the shelf, that's great. Otherwise, just dust around the equipment.

Step 3: Remove any items sitting on top of the bookcase.

Step 4: Spray the dusting cloth with the furniture polish and then clean the top and sides of the bookcase—also dust in front of the books.

Step 5: Put back the things that belong on top of the bookcase and put anything else back where it belongs.

Step 6: Repeat Steps 3, 4, and 5 until all the furniture has been dusted. If your dining table has a glass top, use the glass cleaner.

Step 7: Vacuum the entryway, the couch (lift off the cushions and give them a good plumping up), the rug, and under the table.

Step 8: Put the cleaning supplies away.

Clean the Kitchen

Time allotted: 30-40 minutes

Bring all the cleaning supplies you need into the kitchen.
- Vacuum
- Paper Towels
- All purpose antibacterial cleaner
- Bucket
- Mop
- Sponge
- Cloth for drying (old athletic socks are very absorbent and handy to use.)

I realize that you probably wipe down the counters every time you use them. This is a deeper cleaning that targets the areas you do not wipe down regularly.

Fill the bucket about 1/3 of the way with warm water. Add some of the antibacterial cleaner to the water. Use this water and a sponge to wash with.

Steps to Follow:

Step 1: Take the dish rack and drip pan off the counter.

Step 2: Wash the counter and then dry it.

Step 3: Wash the dish rack and drip pan. Dry the underside of the drip pan and then put both items back on the counter.

Step 4: Clean the top, front, sides, and inside of the microwave.

Step 5: Remove the rings and the drip pans from around the electric coils or gas burner on the stovetop.

Step 6: Fill the sink with hot water and soap. Put the rings and drip pans in the sink to soak.

Step 7: Clean the stovetop.

Step 8: Clean the counter on either side of the stovetop and dry them.

If there are things there that do not belong, put them in a staging area outside the kitchen. When you have finished cleaning the kitchen put those items away.

Step 9: Clean the top, front, and sides of the refrigerator. Take a quick look inside. If there are spills, wipe them up. If there is food that is too old, throw it out (see Chapter Three for guidelines).

Step 10: Wash and dry the drip pans and rings and put them back on the stovetop. Spray a little glass cleaner on a paper towel and wipe off the knobs that control the stovetop and oven—sometimes they get a little goopy.

Step 11: Vacuum the kitchen floor and then mop it.

Step 12: Put the cleaning things away and put away any miscellaneous items that you found on the counters that did not belong in the kitchen.

Appendix F

Maintenance Strategies for Your Computer

Part of Nick's evening routine is to perform some kind of maintenance on our computers. We all depend on our computers to manage our contacts, our calendars, our finances, our jobs, and our communication. I bet you didn't know that the expected useful life of a PC, whether Microsoft Windows-based or Apple OS X-based, is about three years. Desktop models may last a little longer than laptops because they are more durable. The reason for a computer's short life span is that older hardware isn't able to handle newer programs. After three years, component failures, device conflicts, software conflicts, and capacity issues are likely to arise with little or no warning. Here are Nick's suggestions on how to take care of your computer to ensure that it lasts as long as it should, works as efficiently as it can, and safeguards your personal data.

Protect Your Computer from Malware

Malware refers to computer viruses and other malicious programs and documents that can damage your computer, compromise your personal data, or secretly hijack your computer and use it to spread the malware to other computers. Because of its commanding market share, Microsoft Windows is the target of the majority of malware. For that reason, it is particularly important that you take steps to protect your computer if you use it to access the Internet or email. In addition to being careful about opening unknown email attachments and ensuring that any online retail and financial transactions are handled securely, the following steps can safeguard your data and personal information.

For all computers:
1. Do not open email attachments from anyone you don't know. Viruses and other malware are often distributed through spam messages with attachments that look benign but will infect your computer if you open them
2. Be careful about clicking on links in email. A link in email may look like it points to a site you use, but it may be programmed to send you to a malicious site instead. You can eliminate this risk by manually typing the URL into your browser instead of clicking the email link.

For Microsoft Windows:
1. Install all Microsoft-recommended Windows security updates. Windows may be set to do this automatically.
2. Install a high-quality security suite (antivirus, firewall, and spyware) such as Trend Micro Internet Security, AVG Internet Security, or Norton Internet Security. It's critical to keep the definitions and program updates current (they usually update automatically) and to allow the program to run scheduled scans.

For Apple OS X:
1. Install all operating system and security updates. OS X will notify you when updates are available, or you can check manually with the "Software Update..." option under the Apple menu.
2. Disable Java in your web browser unless you are browsing sites that require it.

3. Although Apple computers are less likely to be targets of malware than Windows computers, you can increase your security with free tools like Sophos Antivirus for Mac or ClamXav.

Clean Out Your Cookies, Cache, and History

Cookies are small bits of data that websites store on your computer. They have useful purposes—like remembering your login name the next time you visit a site—but they could be used to compromise your privacy if someone else gets a hold of your computer. The cache is where your computer stores temporary Internet files, and over time it can grow to take up a lot of disk space. Your web browser's history includes links to all of the websites you have recently visited, and deleting it is another way to protect your Internet privacy. You may be able to manage your cookies, cache, and history through your web browser, but it may be easier to use a free program that manages these tasks for you.

For Microsoft Windows:
Install a free cleaner utility such as Piriform's CCleaner and run it daily. It will clean out your cache, cookies, and history, and it also includes a Windows registry cleaner to correct conflicts that may develop within the operating system and between the operating system and installed applications.

For Mac OS X:
Free tools like Titanium Software's OnyX or Maintain's Cocktail include a wide range of system maintenance functionality including cookie, cache, and history deletion.

Back Up Your Hard Drive

One of the most important computer maintenance tasks is to back up your hard drive. The hard drive in your computer is where all your data is stored—documents, photos, music, applications, and more. If the hard drive should crash or be damaged, it may be impossible to retrieve all of those important files. But if you regularly back up your drive, you ensure that you have a recent copy of all of your data that you can transfer to a new drive or computer.

There are two main ways to back up your hard drive: to a separate external drive or to an online backup service (also known as a cloud backup). There are many cloud backup providers, and if you are interested in using one you should take time to do some online research and find out which one best suits your needs.

If you want to back up your data locally, you'll need to purchase an external hard drive. Hard drives come in two main types: drives with mechanical parts, and solid-state drives that have no moving parts. Mechanical drives have the advantage of lower cost and higher capacity but solid-state drives are much more durable and less likely to crash if the drive is dropped or jostled. You should look at the available options and find a backup drive that meets your needs and budget. The drive should have a capacity greater than that of your computer's drive so that it can store multiple backups without running out of space.

In addition to an external drive, you also need backup software to manage the copying and storage of your backed up files.

Different programs have different backup options, but in general you should make sure that the software is set up to run automatic incremental backups at least once a day.

For Microsoft Windows:

A good backup package is 2BrightSparks' SyncBackSE.

For Apple OS X:

The operating system's built-in Time Machine backup application makes it easy to back up your computer without any third-party software.

Note: *There may be times that you want to back up important files but you don't have access to your backup hard drive—if you have a laptop and are working remotely, for example. In this situation, you could use a cloud backup service, if you have one. A quick and easy alternative is to copy the files to a USB flash drive. Flash drives are small and inexpensive and can be carried around in your pocket or on a keychain, so your important data can travel with you.*

Defragment Your Hard Drive

As a computer's hard drive fills up, the operating system may not be able to find big enough blocks of free space on your hard drive for large files. In this case, it may break the files into multiple chunks and store them in different locations on the drive. This is called fragmentation. A defragmenting program scans through the hard drive and reorganizes the data to keep all pieces of a file in a single contiguous chunk. Keeping the hard drive defragmented can speed up performance and prolong the life of the drive by minimizing the work it must do when accessing files.

Note: *Defragmenting is only necessary for mechanical hard drives. You should not run defragmenting software on solid-state drives.*

For Microsoft Windows:
A program such as Diskeeper 2012 Professional runs automatically in the background to eliminate fragments and organize the drive for speedier read-write access.

For Apple OS X:
Defragmentation is usually not necessary for computers running OS X. The operating system automatically organizes files in such a way that fragmentation is limited.

Appendix G
Digital Maintenance Check list

Basic Maintenance for Digital Equipment

Turn off for an hour or more every 48 hours

At least Weekly:

Run a registry scan
Delete browsing history, internet cache and, and recycle bin
Back-up files to an external drive, to cloud storage or to both
Run a virus scan
Create a system restore point

At least monthly:

Install recommended program updates
Uninstall unused programs
Organize email folders and delete unneeded messages
Organize music, photos and videos
Organize folders and files on your hard drive

At least quarterly:

Clean keyboard, monitor and peripherals
Clean air circulation vents and fan blades

At least annually:

Renew software licenses

About the Author

Diane N. Quintana, CPO®, CPO-CD®, has a BA from Washington University. She started her career as an elementary school teacher, teaching kindergarten and first grade. Diane and her husband Nick moved to Bangkok, Thailand in 1979 and from there to Hong Kong. They returned to Connecticut with their first son, Alex, in 1984. In 1993, the family (which now included second son Andy) moved to Singapore, and they returned a second time to Connecticut in 1997. Juggling frequent international moves, raising a family, and working as a teacher helped Diane develop great habits for staying organized.

In 2005, Diane founded her company DNQ Solutions, LLC. She is a Board Certified Professional Organizer and a Certified Professional Organizer specializing in Chronic Disorganization. She teaches her clients how to become organized and provides them with strategies and solutions for maintaining order in their busy lives. Diane is a member of the National Association of Professional Organizers and the Institute for Challenging Disorganization. She is also the ICD Ambassador Team Coordinator. Diane is proud to be affiliated with Parkaire Consultants, Inc. When she is not busy organizing, Diane loves to work in her garden and to participate in ballroom dance competitions.

Diane lives in Atlanta, Georgia.